EASY COMPOSTING
for
ORGANIC GARDENERS

EASY COMPOSTING
for
ORGANIC GARDENERS

Steve Solomon

Easy Composting for Organic Gardeners
Steve Solomon

Copyright © 2022 by Steve Solomon.

Good Books Publishing
goodbookspub.com

ISBN: 978-1-955289-12-2

Contents

Foreword

Fifteen years ago I was living with my wife and three children in a run-down little brick house in Smyrna, Tennessee. I had started a radio production business three years before, doing everything from script-writing to voice work and editing, but the economic downturn and crash in 2007–8 threw us for a loop. We went from the middle class to being borderline poor. Since I had some artistic talent, I took odd jobs painting portraits and trying to sell paintings, and when that wasn't near enough, I started painting houses for a real estate agent friend. I also started tutoring ESL students at a local college.

Through this time our backyard vegetable garden became more impor-tant than ever before. Since we didn't have the resources to buy much to fix our hard, rocky clay, we scavenged and composted everything we could. I gathered endless bags of fall leaves, got permission to rake up spilled straw from the local Lowe's, brought home buckets of coffee grounds from the espresso shop around the corner and even started burying bones and meat scraps in pits we would cover over and plant in the spring. The necessity of feeding our soil—and our family—on a tight budget gave me the knowledge and experience I needed to later write the book *Compost Everything: The Good Guide to Extreme Composting*.

My approach was one of brutal reductionism. I read book after book and article after article on gardening and composting, then broke down all the lofty schemes and theories into the pure basic methods I needed to grow food. Composting, at its essence, is letting things rot. If you throw organic matter on the ground, nature will recycle it.

While I was doing my many experiments and unwittingly doing the prep work for *Compost Everything*, I read Steve Solomon's *Gardening When it Counts*. It was hugely influential on my own thinking and writing. Steve has the ability to take complicated ideas and make them accessible and practical for backyard gardeners.

In this book on composting, he applies his mind and real-life experience to harnessing the process of decomposition in a way that gives you consistently excellent results. Originally published in 1993, it fell out of print, and I did not get a chance to read it until 2021, when Steve sent me a digital copy. Fortunately, as the owner of Good Books Publishing and equipped with a team of good people, I have a unique superpower: I can now bring books back into print!

Throwing stuff on the ground may be the beginning of the process of composting, but if you follow Steve's advice, the end of the process will give you a large harvest of excellent humus for your garden. Humus may not be everything you need to grow a great garden, but it's close. As Sir Albert Howard wrote in *An Agricultural Testament*:

The effect of humus on the crop is nothing short of profound. The farmers and peasants who live in close touch with Nature can tell by a glance at the crop whether or nut the soil is rich in humus. The habit of the plant then develops something approaching personality; the foliage assumes a characteristic set; the leaves acquire the glow of health; the flowers develop depth of color; the minute morphological characters of the whole of the plant organs become clearer and sharper. Root development is profuse: the active roots exhibit not only turgidity but bloom.

The influence of humus on the plant is not confined to the outward appearance of the various organs. The quality of the produce is also affected. Seeds are better developed, and so yield better crops and also provide live stock with a satisfaction not conferred by the produce of worn-out land. The animals need less food if it comes from fertile soil. Vegetables and fruit grown on land rich in humus are always superior in quality, taste, and keeping power to those raised by other means. The quality of wines, other things being equal, follows the same rule.

Easy Composting for Organic Gardeners will help you get the humus you need to transform your soil and your crops. We are very pleased to put it back in print and I think you will find it a very useful addition to your library and your gardening knowledge.

David The Good
2022

To My Readers

A few special books live on in my mind. These were always enjoyable reading. The author's words seemed to speak directly to me like a good friend's conversation pouring from their eyes, heart and soul. When I write I try to make the same thing happen for you. I imagine that there is an audience hearing my words, seated in invisible chairs behind my word processor. You are part of that group. I visualize you as solidly as I can. I create by talking to you.

It helps me to imagine that you are friendly, accepting, and understand my ideas readily. Then I relax, enjoy writing to you and proceed with an open heart. Most important, when the creative process has been fun, the writing still sparkles when I polish it up the next day.

I wrote my first garden book for an audience of one: what seemed a very typical neighbor, someone who only thought he knew a great deal about raising vegetables. Constitutionally, he would only respect and learn from a capital "A" authority who would direct him step-by-step as a cookbook recipe does. So that is what I pretended to be. The result was a concise, basic regional guide to year-round vegetable production. Giving numerous talks on gardening and teaching master gardener classes improved my subsequent books. With this broadening, I expanded my imaginary audience and filled the invisible chairs with all varieties of gardeners who had differing needs and goals.

This particular book gives me an audience problem. Simultaneously I have two quite different groups of composters in mind. What one set wants the other might find boring or even irritating. The smaller group includes serious food gardeners like me. Vegetable gardeners have traditionally been acutely interested in composting, soil building, and maintaining soil organic matter. We are willing to consider anything that might help us grow a better garden and we enjoy agricultural science at a lay person's level.

The other larger audience, does not grow food at all, or if they do it is only a few tomato plants in a flower bed. A few are apartment dwellers who, at best, keep a few house plants. Yet even renters may want to live with greater environmental responsibility by avoiding unnecessary contributions of kitchen garbage to the sewage treatment system. Similarly, modern home owners want to stop sending yard wastes to landfills. These days householders may be offered incentives (or threatened with penalties) by their municipalities to separate organic, compostable garbage from paper, from glass, from metal or from plastic. Individuals who pay for trash pickup by volume are finding that they can save considerable amounts of money by recycling their own organic wastes at home.

The first audience is interested in learning about the role of compost in soil fertility, better soil management methods and growing healthier, more nutritious food. Much like a serious home bread baker, audience one seeks exacting composting recipes that might result in higher quality. Audience two primarily wants to know the easiest and most convenient way to reduce and recycle organic debris.

Holding two conflicting goals at once is the fundamental definition of a problem. Not being willing to abandon either (or both) goals is what keeps a problem alive. The different and somewhat opposing needs of these two audiences make this book somewhat of a problem. To compensate I have positioned complex composting methods and the connections between soil fertility and plant health toward the back of the book. The first two-thirds may be more than sufficient for the larger, more casual members of my imaginary audience. But I could not entirely divide the world of composting into two completely separate levels.

Instead, I tried to write a book so interesting that readers who do not food garden will still want to read it to the end and will realize that there are profound benefits from at-home food production. These run the gamut from physical and emotional health to enhanced economic liberty.

Even if it doesn't seem to specifically apply to your recycling needs, it is my hope that you will become more interested in growing some of your own food. I believe we would have a stronger, healthier and saner country if more liberty-loving Americans would grow food gardens.

Steve Solomon

Part I

Elementary Backyard Composting

Chapter 1

What Is Compost?

Do you know what really happens when things rot? Have other garden books confused you with vague meanings for words like "stabilized humus?" This book won't. Are you afraid that compost making is a nasty, unpleasant, or difficult process? It isn't.

A compost pile is actually a fast-track method of changing crude organic materials into something resembling soil, called humus. But the word "humus" is often misunderstood, along with the words "compost," and "organic matter." And when fundamental ideas like these are not really defined in a person's mind, the whole subject they are a part of may be confused. So this chapter will clarify these basics.

Compost making is a simple process. Done properly it becomes a natural part of your gardening or yard maintenance activities, as much so as mowing the lawn. And making compost does not have to take any more effort than bagging up yard waste.

Handling well-made compost is always a pleasant experience. It is easy to disregard compost's vulgar origins because there is no similarity between the good-smelling brown or black crumbly substance dug out of a compost pile and the manure, garbage, leaves, grass clippings and other waste products from which it began.

Precisely defined, composting means "enhancing the consumption of crude organic matter by a complex ecology of biological decomposition organisms." As raw organic materials are eaten and re-eaten by many, many tiny organisms from bacteria (the smallest) to earthworms (the largest), their components are gradually altered and recombined. Gardeners often use the terms organic matter, compost, and humus as interchangeable identities. But there are important differences in meaning that need to be explained.

This stuff, this organic matter we food gardeners are vitally concerned about, is formed by growing plants that manufacture the substances of life. Most organic molecules are very large, complex assemblies while inorganic materials are much simpler. Animals can break down, reassemble and destroy organic matter but they cannot create it. Only plants can make organic materials like cellulose, proteins, and sugars from inorganic minerals derived from soil, air or water. The elements plants build with include calcium, magnesium, potassium, phosphorus, sodium, sulfur, iron, zinc, cobalt, boron, manganese, molybdenum, carbon, nitrogen, oxygen, and hydrogen.

So organic matter from both land and sea plants fuels the entire chain of life from worms to whales. Humans are most familiar with large animals; they rarely consider that the soil is also filled with animal life busily consuming organic matter or each other. Rich earth abounds with single cell organisms like bacteria, actinomycetes, fungi, protozoa, and rotifers. Soil lifeforms increase in complexity to microscopic round worms called nematodes, various kinds of molluscs like snails and slugs (many so tiny the gardener has no idea they are populating the soil), thousands of almost microscopic soil-dwelling members of the spider family that zoologists call arthropods, the insects in all their profusion and complexity, and, of course, certain larger soil animals most of us are familiar with such as moles. The entire sum of all this organic matter: living plants, decomposing plant materials, and all the animals, living or dead, large and small is sometimes called *biomass.* One realistic way to gauge the fertility of any particular soil body is to weigh the amount of biomass it sustains.

Humus is a special and very important type of decomposed organic matter. Although scientists have been intently studying humus for a century or more, they still do not know its chemical formula. It is certain that humus does not have a single chemical structure, but is a very complex mixture of similar substances that vary according to the types of organic matter that decayed, and the environmental conditions and specific organisms that made the humus.

Whatever its varied chemistry, all humus is brown or black, has a fine, crumbly texture, is very light-weight when dry, and smells like fresh earth. It is sponge-like, holding several times its weight in water. Like clay, humus attracts plant nutrients like a magnet so they aren't so easily washed away by rain or irrigation. Then humus feeds nutrients back to plants. In the words of soil science, this functioning like a storage battery for minerals is called cation exchange capacity. More about that later.

Most important, humus is the last stage in the decomposition of organic matter. Once organic matter has become humus it resists further decomposition. Humus rots slowly. When humus does get broken down by soil microbes it stops being organic matter and changes back to simple inorganic substances. This ultimate destruction of organic matter is often called nitrification because one of the main substances released is nitrate, that vital fertilizer that makes plants grow green and fast.

Probably without realizing it, many non-gardeners have already scuffed up that thin layer of nearly pure humus forming naturally on the forest floor where leaves and needles contact the soil. Most Americans would be repelled by many of the substances that decompose into humus. But, fastidious as we tend to be, most would not be offended to bare-handedly cradle a scoop of humus, raise it to the nose, and take an enjoyable sniff. There seems to be something built into the most primary nature of humans that likes humus.

In nature, the formation of humus is a slow and constant process that does not occur in a single step. Plants grow, die and finally fall to earth where soil-dwelling organisms consume them and each other until eventually there remains no recognizable trace of the original plant. Only a small amount of humus is left, located close to the soil's surface or carried to the depths by burrowing earthworms. Alternately, the growing plants are eaten by animals that do not live in the soil, whose manure falls to the ground where it comes into contact with soil-dwelling organisms that eat it and each other until there remains no recognizable trace of the original material. A small amount of humus is left. Or the animal itself eventually dies and falls to the earth where...

Composting artificially accelerates the decomposition of crude organic matter and its recombination into humus. What in nature might take years we can make happen in weeks or months. But compost that seems ready to work into soil may not have quite yet become humus. Though brown and crumbly and good-smelling and well decomposed, it may only have partially rotted.

When tilled into soil at that point, compost doesn't act at once like powerful fertilizer and won't immediately contribute to plant growth until it has decomposed further. But if composting is allowed to proceed until virtually all of the organic matter has changed into humus, a great deal of biomass will be reduced to a relatively tiny remainder of a very valuable substance far more useful than chemical fertilizer.

For thousands of years gardeners and farmers had few fertilizers other than animal manure and compost. These were always considered very valuable substances and a great deal of lore existed about using them. During the early part of this century our focus changed to using chemicals, and organic wastes were often considered nuisances with little value. These days we are rediscovering compost as an agent of soil improvement and also finding out that we must compost organic waste materials to recycle them in an ecologically sound manner.

Making Compost

The closest analogies to composting I can imagine are concocting similar fermented products like bread, beer, or sauerkraut. But composting is much less demanding. Here I can speak with authority, for during my era of youthful indiscretions I made homebrews good enough have visitors around my kitchen table most every evening. Now, having reluctantly been instructed in moderation by a liver somewhat bruised from alcohol, I am the family baker who turns out two or three large, rye/wheat loaves from freshly ground grain every week without fail.

Brew is dicey. Everything must be sterilized and the fermentation must go rapidly in a narrow range of temperatures. Should stray organisms find a home during fermentation, foul flavors and/or terrible hangovers may result. The wise homebrewer starts with the purest and best-suited strain of yeast a professional laboratory can supply. Making beer is a process suited to the precisionist mentality: it must be done *just so*. Fortunately, with each batch we use the same malt extracts, the same hops, same yeast, same flavorings and, if we are young and foolish, the same monosaccharides to boost the octane over six percent. Once the formula is found and the materials worked out, batch after batch comes out as desired.

So it is with bread-making. The ingredients are standardized and repeatable. I can inexpensively buy several bushels of wheat and rye berries at one time, enough to last a year. Each sack from that purchase has the same baking qualities. The minor ingredients that modify my dough's qualities or the bread's flavors are also repeatable. My yeast is always the same; if I use sourdough starter, my individualized blend of wild yeasts remains the same from batch to batch and I soon learn its nature. My rising oven is always close to the same temperature; when baking I soon learn to adjust the oven temperature and baking time to produce the kind of crust and doneness I desire. Precisionist, yes. I must bake every batch identically if I want the breads to be uniformly good. But not impossibly rigorous because once I learn my materials and oven, I've got it down pat.

Composting is similar, but different and easier. Similar in that decomposition is much like any other fermentation. Different in that the home composter rarely has exactly the same materials to work with from batch to batch, does not need to control the purity and nature of the organisms that will do the actual work of humus formation, and has a broad selection of materials that can go into a batch of compost. Easier because critical and fussy people don't eat or drink compost, the soil does; soil and most plants will, within broad limits, happily tolerate wide variations in compost quality without complaint.

Some composters are very fussy and much like fine bakers or skilled brewers, taking great pains to produce a material exactly to their liking by using complex methods. Usually these are food gardeners with powerful concerns about health, the nutritional quality of the food they grow and the improved growth of their vegetables. However, there are numerous simpler, less rigorous ways of composting that produce a product nearly as good with much less work. These more basic methods will appeal to the less-committed backyard gardener or the homeowner with lawn, shrubs, and perhaps a few flower beds. One unique method suited to handling kitchen garbage—vermicomposting, AKA worm composting—might appeal even to the ecologically concerned apartment dweller with a few house plants.

An Extremely Crude Composting Process

I've been evolving a personally-adapted composting system for the past twenty years. I've gone through a number of methods. I've used and then abandoned power chipper/shredders, used home-made bins and then switched to crude heaps; I've sheet composted, mulched, and used green manure. I first made compost on a half-acre lot where maintaining a tidy appearance was a reasonable concern. Now, living in the country, I don't have be concerned with what the neighbors think of my heaps because the nearest neighbor's house is 800 feet from my compost area and I live in the country because I don't much care to care what my neighbors think.

That's why I now compost so crudely. There are a lot of refinements I could use but don't bother with at this time. I still get fine compost. What follows should be understood as a description of my unique, personal method adapted to my temperament and the climate I live in. I start this book off with such a simple example because I want you to see how completely easy it can be to make perfectly usable compost. I intend this description for inspiration, not emulation.

I am a serious food gardener. Starting in spring I begin to accumulate large quantities of vegetation that demand handling. There are woody stumps and stalks of various members of the cabbage family that usually overwinter in western Oregon's mild winters. These biennials go into bloom by April and at that point I pull them from the garden with a fair amount of soil adhering to the roots. These rough materials form the bottom layer of a new pile.

Since the first principle of abundant living is to produce two or three times as much as you think you'll need, my overly-large garden yields dozens and dozens of such stumps and still more dozens of uneaten savoy cabbages, more dozens of three foot tall Brussels sprouts stalks and cart loads of enormous blooming kale plants. At the same time, from our insulated but unheated garage comes buckets and boxes of sprouting potatoes and cart loads of moldy uneaten winter squashes. There may be a few crates of last fall's withered apples as well. Sprouting potatoes, mildewed squash, and shriveled apples are spread atop the base of brassica stalks.

I grow my own vegetable seed whenever possible, particularly for biennials such as brassicas, beets and endive. During summer these generate large quantities of compostable straw after the seed is thrashed. Usually there is a big dry bean patch that also produces a lot of straw. There are vegetable trimmings, and large quantities of plant material when old spring-sown beds are finished and the soil is replanted for fall harvest. With the first frost in October there is a huge amount of garden clean up.

As each of these materials is acquired it is temporarily placed next to the heap awaiting the steady outpourings from our 2½ gallon kitchen compost pail. Our household generates quite a bit of garbage, especially during high summer when we are canning or juicing our crops. But we have no flies or putrid garbage smells coming from the compost pile because as each bucketful is spread over the center of the pile the garbage is immediately covered by several inches of dried or wilted vegetation and a sprinkling of soil.

By October the heap has become about six feet high, sixteen feet long and about seven feet wide at the base. I've made no attempt to water this pile as it was built, so it is quite dry and has hardly decomposed at all. Soon those famed Maritime northwest winter rains arrive. From mid-October through mid-April it drizzles almost every day and rains fairly hard on occasion. Some 45 inches of water fall. But the pile is loosely stacked with lots of air spaces within and much of the vegetation started the winter in a dry, mature form with a pretty hard "bark" or skin that resists decomposition. Winter days average in the high 40s, so little rotting occurs.

Still, by next April most of the pile has become quite wet. Some garbagey parts of it have decomposed significantly, others not at all; most of it is still quite recognizable but much of the vegetation has a grayish coating of microorganisms or has begun to turn light brown. Now comes the only two really hard hours of compost-making effort each year. For a good part of one morning I turn the pile with a manure fork and shovel, constructing a new pile next to the old one.

First I peel off the barely-rotted outer four or five inches from the old pile; this makes the base of the new one. Untangling the long stringy grasses, seed stalks, and Brussels sprout stems from the rest can make me sweat and even curse, but fortunately I must stop occasionally to spray water where the material remains dry and catch my wind. Then, I rearrange the rest so half-decomposed brassica stumps and other big chunks are placed in the center where the pile will become the hottest and decomposition will proceed most rapidly. As I reform the material, here and there I lightly sprinkle a bit of soil shoveled up from around the original pile. When I've finished turning it, the new heap is about five feet high, six feet across at the bottom, and about eight feet long. The outside is then covered with a thin layer of crumbly, black soil scraped up where the pile had originally stood before I turned it.

Using hand tools for most kinds of garden work, like weeding, cultivating, tilling, and turning compost heaps is not as difficult or nearly as time consuming as most people think if one has the proper, sharp tools. Unfortunately, the knowledge of how to use hand tools has largely disappeared. No one has a farm-bred grandfather to show them how easy it is to use a sharp shovel or how impossibly hard it can be to drive a dull one into the soil. Similarly, weeding with a *sharp* hoe is effortless and fast. But most new hoes are sold without even a proper bevel ground into the blade, much less with an edge that has been carefully honed. So after working with dull shovels and hoes, many home food growers mistakenly conclude that cultivation is not possible without using a rotary tiller for both tillage and weeding between rows. But instead of an expensive gasoline-powered machine all they really needed was a little knowledge and a two dollar file.

Similarly, turning compost can be an impossible, sweat-drenching, back-wrenching chore, or it can be relatively quick and easy. It is very difficult to drive even a very sharp shovel into a compost pile. One needs a hay fork, something most people call a "pitchfork." The best type for this task has a very long, delicate handle and four, foot long, sharp, thin tines. Forks with more than four times grab too much material. If the heap has not rotted very thoroughly and still contains a lot of long, stringy material, a five or six tine fork will grab too much and may require too much strength. Spading forks with four wide-flat blades don't work well for turning heaps, but *in extremis* I'd prefer one to a shovel.

Also, there are shovels and then, there are shovels. Most gardeners know the difference between a spade and a shovel. They would not try to pick up and toss material with a spade designed only to work straight down and loosen soil. However, did you know that there are design differences in the shape of blade and angle of handle in shovels. The normal "combination" shovel is made for builders to move piles of sand or small gravel. However, use a combination shovel to scrape up loose, fine compost that a fork won't hold and you'll quickly have a sore back from bending over so far. Worse, the combination shovel has a decidedly curved blade that won't scrape up very much with each stroke.

A better choice is a flat-bladed, square-front shovel designed to lift loose, fine-textured materials from hard surfaces. However, even well-sharpened, these tend to stick when they bump into any obstacle. Best is an "irrigator's shovel." This is a lightweight tool looking like an ordinary combination shovel but with a flatter, blunter rounded blade attached to the handle at a much sharper angle, allowing the user to stand straighter when working. *Sharp* irrigator's shovels are perfect for scooping up loosened soil and tossing it to one side, for making trenches or furrows in tilled earth and for scraping up the last bits of a compost heap being turned over.

Once turned, my long-weathered pile heats up rapidly. It is not as hot as piles can cook, but it does steam on chilly mornings for a few weeks. By mid-June things have cooled. The rains have also ceased and the heap is getting dry. It has also sagged considerably. Once more I turn the pile, watering it down with a fine mist as I do so. This turning is much easier as the woody brassica stalks are nearly gone. The chunks that remain as visible entities are again put into the new pile's center; most of the bigger and less-decomposed stuff comes from the outside of the old heap. Much of the material has become brown to black in color and its origins are not recognizable. The heap is now reduced to four feet high, five feet wide, and about six feet long. Again I cover it with a thin layer of soil and this time put a somewhat brittle, recycled sheet of clear plastic over it to hold in the moisture and increase the temperature. Again the pile briefly heats and then mellows through the summer.

In September the heap is finished enough to use. It is about thirty inches high and has been reduced to less than one-eighth of its starting volume eighteen months ago. What compost I don't spread during fall is protected with plastic from being leached by winter rainfall and will be used next spring. Elapsed time: 18–24 months from start to finish. Total effort: three turnings. Quality: very useful.

Obviously my method is acceptable to me because the pile is not easily visible to the residents or neighbors. It also suits a lazy person. It is a very slow system, okay for someone who is not in a hurry to use their compost. But few of my readers live on really rural properties; hopefully, most of them are not as lazy as I am.

At this point I could recommend alternative, improved methods for making compost much like cookbook recipes from which the reader could pick and choose. There could be a small backyard recipe, the fast recipe, the apartment recipe, the wintertime recipe, the making compost when you can't make a pile recipes. Instead, I prefer to compliment your intelligence and first explore the principles behind composting. I believe that an understanding of basics will enable you to function as a self-determined individual and adapt existing methods, solve problems if they arise, or create something personal and uniquely correct for your situation.

Chapter 2

Composting Basics

Managing living systems usually goes better when our methods imitate nature's. Here's an example of what happens when we don't.

People who keep tropical fish in home aquariums are informed that to avoid numerous fish diseases they must maintain sterile conditions. Whenever the fish become ill or begin dying, the hobbyist is advised to put antibiotics or mild antiseptics into the tank, killing off most forms of microlife. But nature is not sterile. Nature is healthy.

Like many an apartment dweller, in my twenties I raised tropical fish and grew house plants just to have some life around. The plants did fine; I guess I've always had a green thumb. But growing tired of dying fish and bacterial blooms clouding the water, I reasoned that none of the fish I had seen in nature were diseased and their water was usually quite clear. Perhaps the problem was that my aquarium had an overly simplified ecology and my fish were being fed processed, dead food when in nature the ecology was highly complex and the fish were eating living things. So I bravely attempted the most radical thing I could think of; I went to the country, found a small pond and from it brought home a quart of bottom muck and pond water that I dumped into my own aquarium. Instead of introducing countless diseases and wiping out my fish, I actually had introduced countless living things that began multiplying rapidly. The water soon became crystal clear. Soon the fish were refusing to eat the scientifically formulated food flakes I was supplying. The profuse variety of little critters now living in the tank's gravel ate it instead. The fish ate the critters and became perfectly healthy.

When the snails I had introduced with the pond mud became so numerous that they covered the glass and began to obscure my view, I'd crush a bunch of them against the wall of the aquarium and the fish would gorge on fresh snail meat. The angelfish and guppies especially began to look forward to my snail massacres and would cluster around my hand when I put it into the tank. On a diet of living things in a natural ecology even very difficult species began breeding.

Organic and biological farmers consider modern "scientific" farming practices to be a similar situation. Instead of imitating nature's complex stability, industrial farmers use force, attempting to bend an unnaturally simplified ecosystem to their will. As a result, most agricultural districts are losing soil at a non-sustainable rate and produce food of lowered nutritional content, resulting in decreasing health for all the life forms eating the production of our farms. Including us.

I am well aware that these condemnations may sound quite radical to some readers. In a book this brief I cannot offer adequate support for my concerns about soil fertility and the nation's health, but I can refer the reader to the bibliography, where books about these matters by writers far more sagely than I can be found. I especially recommend the works of William Albrecht, Weston Price, Sir Robert McCarrison, and Sir Albert Howard.

Making Humus

Before we ask how to compost, since nature is maximally efficient perhaps it would benefit us to first examine how nature goes about returning organic matter to the soil from whence it came. If we do nearly as well, we can be proud.

Where nature is allowed to operate without human intervention, each place develops a stable level of biomass that is inevitably the highest amount of organic life that site could support. Whether deciduous forest, coniferous forest, prairie, even desert, nature makes the most of the available resources and raises the living drama to its most intense and complex peak possible. There will be as many mammals as there can be, as many insects, as many worms, as many plants growing as large as they can get, as much organic matter in all stages of decomposition and the maximum amount of relatively stable humus in the soil. All these forms of living and decomposing organisms are linked in one complex system; each part so closely connected to all the others that should one be lessened or increased, all the others change as well.

The efficient decomposition of leaves on a forest floor is a fine example of what we might hope to achieve in a compost pile. Under the shade of the trees and mulched thickly by leaves, the forest floor usually stays moist. Although the leaves tend to mat where they contact the soil, the wet, somewhat compacted layer is thin enough to permit air to be in contact with all of the materials and to enter the soil.

The animals that begin the process of humification live in this very top layer of leaf material and humus mixed with fluffy, crumbly, moist soil. Many of these primary decomposers are larger, insect-like animals commonly known to gardeners, including the wood lice that we call pill bugs because they roll up defensively into hard armadillo-like shells, and the highly intrusive earwigs my daughter calls pinch bugs. There are also numerous types of insect larvae busily at work.

A person could spend his entire life trying to understand the ecology of a single handful of humus-rich topsoil. For a century now, numerous soil biologists have been doing just that and still the job is not finished. Since gardeners, much less ordinary people, are rarely interested in observing and naming the tiny animals of the soil, especially are we disinterested in those who do no damage to our crops, soil animals are usually delineated only by Latin scientific names. The variations with which soil animals live, eat, digest, reproduce, attack, and defend themselves fills whole sections of academic science libraries.

During the writing of this book I became quite immersed in this subject and read far more deeply into soil biology and microbiology than I thought I ever would. Even though this area of knowledge has amused me, I doubt it will entertain most of you. If it does, I recommend that you first consult specialist source materials listed in the bibliography for an introduction to a huge universe of literature.

I will not make you yawn by mentioning long, unfamiliar Latin names. I will not astonish you with descriptions of complex reproductive methods and beautiful survival strategies. Gardeners do not really need this information. But managing the earth so that soil animals are helped and not destroyed is essential to good gardening. And there are a few qualities of soil animals that are found in almost all of them. If we are aware of the general characteristics of soil animals we can evaluate our composting and gardening practices by their effect on these minuscule creatures.

Compared to the atmosphere, soil is a place where temperature fluctuations are small and slow. Consequently, soil animals are generally intolerant to sudden temperature changes and may not function well over a very wide range. That's why leaving bare earth exposed to the hot summer sun often retards plant growth and why many thoughtful gardeners either put down a thin mulch in summer or try to rapidly establish a cooling leaf canopy to shade raised beds. Except for a few microorganisms, soil animals breathe oxygen just like other living things and so are dependent on an adequate air supply. Where soil is airless due to compaction, poor drainage, or large proportions of very fine clay, soil animals are few in number.

The soil environment is generally quite moist; even when the soil seems a little dryish the relative humidity of the soil air usually approaches 100 percent. Soil animals consequently have not developed the ability to conserve their body moisture and are speedily killed by dry conditions. When faced with desiccation they retreat deeper into the soil if there is oxygen and pore spaces large enough to move about. So we see another reason why a thin mulch that preserves surface moisture can greatly increase the beneficial population of soil animals. Some single-cell animals and roundworms are capable of surviving stress by encysting themselves, forming a little "seed" that preserves their genetic material and enough food to reactivate it, coming back to life when conditions improve. These cysts may endure long periods of severe freezing and sometimes temperatures of over 150° F.

Inhabitants of leaf litter reside close to the surface and so must be able to experience exposure to dryer air and light for short times without damage. The larger litter livers are called primary decomposers. They spend most of their time chewing on the thick reserve of moist leaves contacting the forest floor. Primary decomposers are unable to digest the entire leaf. They extract only the easily assimilable substances from their food: proteins, sugars and other simple carbohydrates and fats. Cellulose and lignin are the two substances that make up the hard, permanent, and woody parts of plants; these materials cannot be digested by most soil animals. Interestingly, just like in a cow's rumen, there are a few larvae whose digestive tract contains cellulose-decomposing bacteria but these larvae have little overall effect.

After the primary consumers are finished the leaves have been mechanically disintegrated and thoroughly moistened, worked over, chewed to tiny pieces and converted into minuscule bits of moist excrement still containing active digestive enzymes. Many of the bacteria and fungi that were present on the leaf surfaces have passed through this initial digestion process alive or as spores waiting and ready to activate. In this sense, the excrement of the primary decomposers is not very different than manure from large vegetarian mammals like cows and sheep although it is in much smaller pieces.

Digestive wastes of primary decomposers are thoroughly inoculated with microorganisms that can consume cellulose and lignin. Even though it looks like humus, it has not yet fully decomposed. It does have a water-retentive, granular structure that facilitates the presence of air and moisture throughout the mass creating perfect conditions for microbial digestion to proceed.

This excrement is also the food for a diverse group of nearly microscopic soil animals called secondary decomposers. These are incapable of eating anything that has not already been predigested by the primary decomposers. The combination of microbes and the digestive enzymes of the primary and secondary decomposers breaks down resistant cellulose and to some degree, even lignin. The result is a considerable amount of secondary decomposition excrement having a much finer crumb structure than what was left by the primary decomposers. It is closer to being humus but is still not quite finished.

Now comes the final stage in humus formation. Numerous species of earthworms eat their way through the soil, taking in a mixture of earth, microbes, and the excrement of soil animals. All of these substances are mixed together, ground-up, and chemically recombined in the worm's highly active and acidic gut. Organic substances chemically unite with soil to form clay/humus complexes that are quite resistant to further decomposition and have an extraordinarily high ability to hold and release the very nutrients and water that feed plants. Earthworm casts (excrement) are mechanically very stable and help create a durable soil structure that remains open and friable, something gardeners and farmers call good tilth or good crumb. Earthworms are so vitally important to soil fertility and additionally useful as agents of compost making that an entire section of this book will consider them in great detail.

Let's underline a composting lesson to be drawn from the forest floor. In nature, humus formation goes on in the presence of air and moisture. The agents of its formation are soil animals ranging in complexity from microorganisms through insects working together in a complex ecology. These same organisms work our compost piles and help us change crude vegetation into humus or something close to humus. So, when we make compost we need to make sure that there is sufficient air and moisture.

Decomposition is actually a process of repeated digestions as organic matter passes and repasses through the intestinal tracts of soil animals numerous times or is attacked by the digestive enzymes secreted by microorganisms. At each stage the vegetation and decomposition products of that vegetation are thoroughly mixed with animal digestive enzymes. Soil biologists have observed that where soil conditions are hostile to soil animals, such as in compacted fine clay soils that exclude air, organic matter is decomposed exclusively by microorganisms. Under those conditions virtually no decomposition-resistant humus/clay complexes form; almost everything is consumed by the bacterial community as fuel. And the non-productive soil is virtually devoid of organic matter.

Sir Albert Howard has been called the "father of modern composting." His first composting book (1931) *The Waste Products of Agriculture,* stressed the vital importance of animal digestive enzymes from fresh cow manure in making compost. When he experimented with making compost without manure the results were less than ideal. Most gardeners cannot obtain fresh manure but fortunately soil animals will supply similar digestive enzymes. Later on when we review Howard's Indore composting method we will see how brilliantly Sir Albert understood natural decomposition and mimicked it in a composting method that resulted in a very superior product.

At this point I suggest another definition for humus. Humus is the excrement of soil animals, primarily earthworms, but including that of some other species that, like earthworms, are capable of combining partially decomposed organic matter and the excrement of other soil animals with clay to create stable soil crumbs resistant to further decomposition or consumption.

Nutrients in the Compost Pile

Some types of leaves rot much faster on the forest floor than others. Analyzing why this happens reveals a great deal about how to make compost piles decompose more effectively.

Leaves from leguminous (in the same botanical family as beans and peas) trees such as acacia, carob, and alder usually become humus within a year. So do some others like ash, cherry, and elm. More resistant types take two years; these include oak, birch, beech, and maple. Poplar leaves, and pine, Douglas fir, and larch needles are very slow to decompose and may take three years or longer. Some of these differences are due to variations in lignin content which is highly resistant to decomposition, but speed of decomposition is mainly influenced by the amount of protein and mineral nutrients contained in the leaf.

Plants are composed mainly of carbohydrates like cellulose, sugar, and lignin. The element carbon is by far the greater part of carbohydrates [carbo(n)hydr(ogen)ates] by weight. Plants can readily manufacture carbohydrates in large quantities because carbon and hydrogen are derived from air (CO_2) and water (H_2O), both substances being available to plants in almost unlimited quantities.

Sugar, manufactured by photosynthesis, is the simplest and most vital carbohydrate. Sugar is "burned" in all plant cells as the primary fuel powering all living activities. Extra sugar can be more compactly stored after being converted into starches, which are long strings of sugar molecules linked together. Plants often have starch-filled stems, roots, or tubers; they also make enzymes capable of quickly converting this starch back into sugar upon demand. We homebrewers and bakers make practical use of a similar enzyme process to change starches stored in grains back to sugar that yeasts can change into alcohol.

Sometimes plants store food in the form of oil, the most concentrated biological energy source. Oil is also constructed from sugar and is usually found in seeds. Plants also build structural materials like stem, cell walls, and other woody parts from sugars converted into cellulose, a substance similar to starch. Very strong structures are constructed with lignins, a material like cellulose but much more durable. Cellulose and lignins are permanent. They cannot be converted back into sugar by plant enzymes. Nor can most animals or bacteria digest them.

Certain fungi can digest cellulose and lignin, as can the symbiotic bacteria inhabiting a cow's rumen. In this respect the cow is a very clever animal running a cellulose digestion factory in the first and largest of its several stomachs. There, it cultures bacteria that eat cellulose; then the cow digests the bacteria as they pass out of one stomach and into another.

Plants also construct proteins, the vital stuff of life itself. Proteins are mainly found in those parts of the plant involved with reproduction and photosynthesis. Protein molecules differ from starches and sugars in that they are larger and amazingly more complex. Most significantly, while carbohydrates are mainly carbon and hydrogen, proteins contain large amounts of nitrogen and numerous other mineral nutrients.

Proteins are scarce in nature. Plants can make them only in proportion to the amount of the nutrient, nitrogen, that they take up from the soil. Most soils are very poorly endowed with nitrogen. If nitrate-poor, nutrient-poor soil is well-watered there may be lush vegetation but the plants will contain little protein and can support few animals. But where there are high levels of nutrients in the soil there will be large numbers of animals, even if the land is poorly watered and grows only scrubby grasses—verdant forests usually feed only a few shy deer while the short grass semi-desert prairies once supported huge herds of grazing animals.

Ironically, just as it is with carbon, there is no absolute shortage of nitrogen on Earth. The atmosphere is nearly 80 percent nitrogen. But in the form of gas, atmospheric nitrogen is completely useless to plants or animals. It must first be combined chemically into forms plants can use, such as nitrate (NO3) or ammonia (NH3). These chemicals are referred to as "fixed nitrogen."

Nitrogen gas strongly resists combining with other elements. Chemical factories fix nitrogen only at very high temperatures and pressures and in the presence of exotic catalysts like platinum or by exposing nitrogen gas to powerful electric sparks. Lightning flashes can similarly fix small amounts of nitrogen that fall to earth dissolved in rain.

And certain soil-dwelling microorganisms are able to fix atmospheric nitrogen. But these are abundant only where the earth is rich in humus and minerals, especially calcium. So in a soil body where large quantities of fixed nitrogen are naturally present, the soil will also be well-endowed with a good supply of mineral nutrients.

Most of the world's supply of combined nitrogen is biologically fixed at normal temperatures and standard atmospheric pressure by soil microorganisms. We call the ones that live freely in soil "azotobacteria" and the ones that associate themselves with the roots of legumes "rhizobia." Blue-green algae of the type that thrive in rice paddies also manufacture nitrate nitrogen. We really don't know how bacteria accomplish this but the nitrogen they "fix" is the basis of most proteins on earth.

All microorganisms, including nitrogen-fixing bacteria, build their bodies from the very same elements that plants use for growth. Where these mineral elements are abundant in soil, the entire soil body is more alive and carries much more biomass at all levels from bacteria through insects, plants, and even mammals.

Should any of these vital nutrient substances be in short supply, all biomass and plant growth will decrease to the level permitted by the amount available, even though there is an overabundance of all the rest. The name for this phenomena is the "Law of Limiting Factors." The concept of limits was first formulated by a scientist, Justus von Liebig, in the middle of the last century. Although Liebig's name is not popular with organic gardeners and farmers because misconceptions of his ideas have led to the widespread use of chemical fertilizers, Liebig's theory of limits is still good science.

Liebig suggested imagining a barrel being filled with water as a metaphor for plant growth: the amount of water held in the barrel being the amount of growth. Each stave represents one of the factors or requirements plants need in order to grow such as light, water, oxygen, nitrogen, phosphorus, copper, boron, etc. Lowering any one stave of the barrel, no matter which one, lessens the amount of water that can be held and thus growth is reduced to the level of the most limited growth factor.

For example, one essential plant protein is called chlorophyll, the green pigment found in leaves that makes sugar through photosynthesis. Chlorophyll is a protein containing significant amounts of magnesium. Obviously, the plant's ability to grow is limited by its ability to find enough fixed nitrogen and also magnesium to make this protein.

Animals of all sizes from elephants to single cell microorganisms are primarily composed of protein. But the greatest portion of plant material is not protein, it is carbohydrates in one form or another. Eating enough carbohydrates to supply their energy requirements is rarely the survival problem faced by animals; finding enough protein (and other vital nutrients) in their food supply to grow and reproduce is what limits their population. The numbers and health of grazing animals is limited by the protein and other nutrient content of the grasses they are eating, similarly the numbers and health of primary decomposers living on the forest floor is limited by the nutrient content of their food. And so is the rate of decomposition. And so too is this true in the compost pile.

The protein content of vegetation is very similar to its ratio of carbon (C) compared to nitrogen (N). Quick laboratory analysis of protein content is not done by measuring actual protein itself but by measuring the amount of combined nitrogen the protein gives off while decomposing.

C/N Ratio of Tree Leaves & Needles	
False acacia	14:1
Black alder	15:1
Gray alder	19:1
Ash	21:1
Bird's eye cherry	22:1
Hornbeam	23:1
Elm	28:1
Lime	37:1
Oak	47:1
Fir	48:1
Birch	50:1
Beech	51:1
Maple	52:1
Red oak	53:1
Poplar	63:1
Pine	66:1
Douglas fir	77:1
Larch	113:1

Acacia, alder, and leaves of other proteinaceous legumes such as locust, mesquite, scotch broom, vetch, alfalfa, beans, and peas have low C/N ratios because legume roots uniquely can shelter clusters of nitrogen-fixing rhizobia. These microorganisms can supply all the nitrate nitrogen fast-growing legumes can use if the soil is also well endowed with other mineral nutrients rhizobia need, especially calcium and phosphorus. Most other plant families are entirely dependent on nitrate supplies presented to them by the soil. Consequently, those regions or locations with soils deficient in mineral nutrients tend to grow coniferous forests while richer soils support forests with more protein in their leaves. There may also be climatic conditions that favor conifers over deciduous trees, regardless of soil fertility.

It is generally true that organic matter with a high ratio of carbon to nitrogen also will have a high ratio of carbon to other minerals. And low C/N materials will contain much larger amounts of other vital mineral nutrients. When we make compost from a wide variety of materials there are probably enough quantity and variety of nutrients in the plant residues to form large populations of humus-forming soil animals and microorganisms. However, when making compost primarily with high C/N stuff we need to blend in other substances containing sufficient fixed nitrogen and other vital nutrient minerals. Otherwise, the decomposition process will take a very long time because large numbers of decomposing organisms will not be able to develop.

The lists in this table of carbon-to-nitrogen ratios are broken out as general ranges of C/N. It has long been an unintelligent practice of garden-level books to state "precise" C/N ratios for materials. One substance will be 23:1 while another will be 25:1. Such pseudoscience is not only inaccurate but it leads readers into similar misunderstandings about other such lists, like nitrogen contents, or composition breakdowns of organic manures, or other organic soil amendments. Especially misleading are those tables in the back of many health and nutrition books spelling out the "exact" nutrient contents of foods. There is an old saying about this: "There are lies, then there are damned lies, and then, there are statistics. The worse lies of all can be statistics.'

The composition of plant materials is very dependent on the level and nature of the soil fertility that produced them. The nutrition present in two plants of the same species, even in two samples of the exact same variety of vegetable raised from the same packet of seed can vary enormously depending on where the plants were grown. William Albrecht, chairman of the Soil Department at the University of Missouri during the 1930s, was, to the best of my knowledge, the first mainstream scientist to thoroughly explore the differences in the nutritional qualities of plants and to identify specific aspects of soil fertility as the reason why one plant can be much more nutritious than another and why animals can be so much healthier on one farm compared to another. By implication, Albrecht also meant to show the reason why one nation of people can be much

±6:1
Bone Meal • Meat scraps • Fish waste • Rabbit manure • Chicken manure • Pig manure • Seed meal

±12:1
Vegetables • Garden weeds • Alfalfa hay • Horse manure • Sewage sludge • Silage • Cow manure

±25:1
Summer grass • Seaweed • Legume hulls • Fruit waste • Hay (top quality)

±50:1
Cornstalks (dry) • Straw (grain) • Hay (low quality)

±100:1
Sawdust • Paper • Tree bark • Bagasse • Grain chaff • Corn cobs • Cotton mill waste

less healthy than another. Because his holistic outlook ran counter to powerful vested interests of his era, Albrecht was professionally scorned and ultimately left the university community, spending the rest of his life educating the general public, especially farmers and health care professionals.

Summarized in one paragraph, Albrecht showed that within a single species or variety, plant protein levels vary 25 percent or more depending on soil fertility, while a plant's content of vital nutrients like calcium, magnesium, and phosphorus can simultaneously move up or down as much as 300 percent, usually corresponding to similar changes in its protein level. Albrecht also discovered how to manage soil in order to produce highly nutritious food. Chapter 8 has a lot more praise for Dr. Albrecht. There I explore this interesting aspect of gardening in more detail because how we make and use organic matter has a great deal to do with the resulting nutritional quality of the food we grow.

Imagine trying to make compost from deficient materials such as a heap of pure, moist sawdust. What happens? Very little and very, very slowly. Trees locate most of their nutrient accumulation in their leaves to make protein for photosynthesis. A small amount goes into making bark. Wood itself is virtually pure cellulose, derived from air and water. If, when we farmed trees, we removed only the wood and left the leaves and bark on the site, we would be removing next to nothing from the soil. If the sawdust comes from a lumber mill, as opposed to a cabinet shop, it may also contain some bark and consequently small amounts of other essential nutrients.

Thoroughly moistened and heaped up, a sawdust pile would not heat up, only a few primary decomposers would take up residence. A person could wait five years for compost to form from pure moist sawdust and still not much would happen. Perhaps that's why the words "compost" and "compot" as the British mean it, are connected. In England, a compot is a slightly fermented mixture of many things like fruits. If we mixed the sawdust with other materials having a very low C/N, then it would decompose, along with the other items.

Chapter 3

Practical Compost Making

To make compost rot rapidly you need to achieve a strong and lasting rise in temperature. Cold piles will eventually decompose and humus will eventually form but, without heat, the process can take a long, long time. Getting a pile to heat up promptly and stay hot requires the right mixture of materials and a sensible handling of the pile's air and moisture supply.

Compost piles come with some built-in obstacles. The intense heat and biological activity make a heap slump into an airless mass, yet if composting is to continue the pile must allow its living inhabitants sufficient air to breath. Hot piles tend to dry out rapidly, but must be kept moist or they stop working. But heat is desirable and watering cools a pile down. If understood and managed, these difficulties are really quite minor.

Composting is usually an inoffensive activity, but if done incorrectly there can be problems with odor and flies. This chapter will show you how to make nuisance-free compost.

Hot Composting

The main difference between composting in heaps and natural decomposition on the earth's surface is temperature. On the forest floor, leaves leisurely decay and the primary agents of decomposition are soil animals. Bacteria and other microorganisms are secondary. In a compost pile the opposite occurs: we substitute a violent fermentation by microorganisms such as bacteria and fungi. Soil animals are secondary and come into play only after the microbes have had their hour.

Under decent conditions, with a relatively unlimited food supply, bacteria, yeasts, and fungi can double their numbers every twenty to thirty minutes, increasing geometrically: 1, 2, 4, 8, 16, 32, 64, 128, 256, 512, 1,024, 2,048, etc. In only four hours one cell multiplies to over four thousand. In three more hours there will be two million.

For food, they consume the compost heap. Almost all oxygen-breathing organisms make energy by "burning" some form of organic matter as fuel much like gasoline powers an automobile. This cellular burning does not happen violently with flame and light. Living things use enzymes to break complex organic molecules down into simpler ones like sugar (and others) and then enzymatically unite these with oxygen. But as gentle as enzymatic combustion may seem, it still is burning. Microbes can "burn" starches, cellulose, lignin, proteins, and fats, as well as sugars.

No engine is one hundred percent efficient. All motors give off waste heat as they run. Similarly, no plant or animal is capable of using every bit of energy released from their food, and consequently radiate heat. When working hard, living things give off more heat; when resting, less. The ebb and flow of heat production matches their oxygen consumption, and matches their physical and metabolic activities, and growth rates. Even single-celled animals like bacteria and fungi breathe oxygen and give off heat.

Soil animals and microorganisms working over the thin layer of leaf litter on the forest floor also generate heat but it dissipates without making any perceptible increase in temperature. However, compostable materials do not transfer heat readily. In the language of architecture and home building they might be said to have a high "R" value or to be good insulators When a large quantity of decomposing materials are heaped up, biological heat is trapped within the pile and temperature increases, further accelerating the rate of decomposition.

Temperature controls how rapidly living things carry out their activities. Only birds and mammals are warm blooded-capable of holding the rate of their metabolic chemistry constant by holding their body temperature steady. Most animals and all microorganisms have no ability to regulate their internal temperature; when they are cold they are sluggish, when warm, active. Driven by cold-blooded soil animals and microorganisms, the hotter the compost pile gets the faster it is consumed.

This relationship between temperature and the speed of biological activity also holds true for organic chemical reactions in a test-tube, the shelf-life of garden seed, the time it takes seed to germinate and the storage of food in the refrigerator. At the temperature of frozen water most living chemical processes come to a halt or close to it. That is why freezing prevents food from going through those normal enzymatic decomposition stages we call spoiling.

By the time that temperature has increased to about 50° F, the chemistry of most living things is beginning to operate efficiently. From that temperature the speed of organic chemical reactions then approximately doubles with each 20 degree increase of temperature. So, at 70° F decomposition is running at twice the rate it does at 50°, while at 90° four times as rapidly as at 50° and so on. However, when temperatures get to about 150° organic chemistry is not necessarily racing 32 times as fast as compared to 50° because many reactions engendered by living things decline in efficiency at temperatures much over 110°.

This explanation is oversimplified and the numbers I have used to illustrate the process are slightly inaccurate, however the idea itself is substantially correct. You should understand that while inorganic chemical reactions accelerate with increases in temperature almost without limit, those processes conducted by living things usually have a much lower terminal temperature. Above some point, life stops. Even the most heat tolerant soil animals will die or exit a compost pile by the time the temperature exceeds 120°, leaving the material in the sole possession of microorganisms.

Most microorganisms cannot withstand temperatures much over 130°. When the core of a pile heats beyond this point they either form spores while waiting for things to cool off, or die off. Plenty of living organisms will still be waiting in the cooler outer layers of the heap to reoccupy the core once things cool down. However, there are unique bacteria and fungi that only work effectively at temperatures exceeding 110°. Soil scientists and other academics that sometimes seem to measure their stature on how well they can baffle the average person by using unfamiliar words for ordinary notions call these types of organisms *thermophiles,* a Latin word that simply means "heat lovers."

Compost piles can get remarkably hot. Since thermophilic microorganisms and fungi generate the very heat they require to accelerate their activities and as the ambient temperature increases generate even more heat, the ultimate temperature is reached when the pile gets so hot that even thermophilic organisms begin to die off. Compost piles have exceeded 160°. You should expect the heaps you build to exceed 140° and shouldn't be surprised if they approach 150°

Other types of decomposing organic matter can get even hotter. For example, haystacks commonly catch on fire because dry hay is such an excellent insulator. If the bales in the center of a large hay stack are just moist enough to encourage rapid bacterial decomposition, the heat generated may increase until dryer bales on the outside begin to smoke and then burn. Wise farmers make sure their hay is thoroughly dry before baling and stacking it.

How hot the pile can get depends on how well the composter controls a number of factors. These are so important that they need to be considered in detail.

Particle size
Microorganisms are not capable of chewing or mechanically attacking food. Their primary method of eating is to secrete digestive enzymes that break down and then dissolve organic matter. Some larger single-cell creatures can surround or envelop and then "swallow" tiny food particles. Once inside the cell this material is then attacked by similar digestive enzymes.

Since digestive enzymes attack only outside surfaces, the greater the surface area the composting materials present the more rapidly microorganisms multiply to consume the food supply. And the more heat is created. As particle size decreases, the amount of surface area goes up just about as rapidly as the number series used a few paragraphs back to illustrate the multiplication of microorganisms.

The surfaces presented in different types of soil similarly affect plant growth so scientists have carefully calculated the amount of surface areas of soil materials. Although compost heaps are made of much larger particles than soil, the relationship between particle size and surface area is the same. Clearly, when a small difference in particle size can change the amount of surface area by hundreds of times, reducing the size of the stuff in the compost pile will:

- expose more material to digestive enzymes;

- greatly accelerate decomposition;

- build much higher temperatures.

Oxygen supply

All desirable organisms of decomposition are oxygen breathers or aerobes. There must be an adequate movement of air through the pile to supply their needs. If air supply is choked off, aerobic microorganisms die off and are replaced by anaerobic organisms. These do not run by burning carbohydrates, but derive energy from other kinds of chemical reactions not requiring oxygen. Anaerobic chemistry is slow and does not generate much heat, so a pile that suddenly cools off is giving a strong indication that the core may lack air. The primary waste products of aerobes are water and carbon dioxide gas—inoffensive substances. When most people think of putrefaction they are actually picturing decomposition by anaerobic bacteria. With insufficient oxygen, foul-smelling materials are created. Instead of humus being formed, black, tar-like substances develop that are much less useful in soil. Under airless conditions much nitrate is permanently lost. The odiferous wastes of anaerobes also includes hydrogen sulfide (smells like rotten eggs), as well as other toxic substances with very unpleasant qualities.

Heaps built with significant amounts of coarse, strong, irregular materials tend to retain large pore spaces, encourage airflow and remain aerobic. Heat generated in the pile causes hot air in the pile's center to rise and exit the pile by convection. This automatically draws in a supply of fresh, cool air. But heaps made exclusively of large particles not only present little surface area to microorganisms, they permit so much airflow that they are rapidly cooled. This is one reason that a wet firewood rick or a pile of damp wood chips does not heat up. At the opposite extreme, piles made of finely ground or soft, wet materials tend to compact, ending convective air exchanges and bringing aerobic decomposition to a halt. In the center of an airless heap, anaerobic organisms immediately take over.

Surface Area of One Gram of Soil Particles

Particle type	Diameter in mm	Particles/gm	Surface (cm^2)
Very coarse sand	2.00–1.00	90	11
Coarse sand	1.00–0.50	720	23
Medium sand	0.50–0.25	5,700	45
Fine sand	0.25–0.10	46,000	91
Very fine sand	0.10–0.05	772,000	227
Silt	0.05–0.002	5,776,000	454

Composters use several strategies to maintain airflow. The most basic one is to blend an assortment of components so that coarse, stiff materials maintain a loose texture while soft, flexible stuff tends to partially fill in the spaces. However, even if the heap starts out fluffy enough to permit adequate airflow, as the materials decompose they soften and tend to slump together into an airless mass.

Periodically turning the pile, tearing it apart with a fork and restacking it, will reestablish a looser texture and temporarily recharge the pore spaces with fresh air. Since the outer surfaces of a compost pile do not get hot, tend to completely dry out, and fail to decompose, turning the pile also rotates the unrotted skin to the core and then insulates it with more-decomposed material taken from the center of the original pile. A heap that has cooled because it has gone anaerobic can be quickly remedied by turning.

Piles can also be constructed with a base layer of fine sticks, smaller tree prunings, and dry brushy material. This porous base tends to enhance the inflow of air from beneath the pile. One powerful aeration technique is to build the pile atop a low platform made of slats or strong hardware cloth.

Larger piles can have air channels built into them much as light wells and courtyards illuminate inner rooms of tall buildings. As the pile is being constructed, vertical heavy wooden fence posts, 4 x 4's, or large-diameter plastic pipes with numerous quarter-inch holes drilled in them are spaced every three or four feet. Once the pile has been formed and begins to heat, the wooden posts are wiggled around and then lifted out, making a slightly conical airway from top to bottom. Perforated plastic vent pipes can be left in the heap. With the help of these airways, no part of the pile is more than a couple of feet from oxygen.

Moisture

A dry pile is a cold pile. Microorganisms live in thin films of water that adhere to organic matter whereas fungi only grow in humid conditions; if the pile becomes dry, both bacteria and fungi die off. The upwelling of heated air exiting the pile tends to rapidly dehydrate the compost heap. It usually is necessary to periodically add water to a hot working heap. Unfortunately, remoistening a pile is not always simple. The nature of the materials tends to cause water to be shed and run off much like a thatched roof protects a cottage.

Since piles tend to compact and dry out at the same time, when they are turned they can simultaneously be rehydrated. When I fork over a heap I take brief breaks and spray water over the new pile, layer by layer. Two or three such turnings and waterings will result in finished compost.

The other extreme can also be an obstacle to efficient composting. Making a pile too wet can encourage soft materials to lose all mechanical strength, the pile immediately slumps into a chilled, airless mass. Having large quantities of water pass through a pile can also leach out vital nutrients that feed organisms of decomposition and later on, feed the garden itself. I cover my heaps with old plastic sheeting from November through March to protect them from Oregon's rainy winter climate.

Understanding how much moisture to put into a pile soon becomes an intuitive certainty. Beginners can gauge moisture content by squeezing a handful of material very hard. It should feel very damp but only a few drops of moisture should be extractable. Industrial composters, who can afford scientific guidance to optimize their activities, try to establish and maintain a laboratory-measured moisture content of 50 to 60 percent by weight. When building a pile, keep in mind that certain materials like fresh grass clippings and vegetable trimmings already contain close to 90 percent moisture while dry components such as sawdust and straw may contain only 10 percent and resist absorbing water at that. But, by thoroughly mixing wet and dry materials the overall moisture content will quickly equalize.

Size of the pile

It is much harder to keep a small object hot than a large one. That's because the ratio of surface area to volume goes down as volume goes up. No matter how well other factors encourage thermophiles, it is still difficult to make a pile heat up that is less than three feet high and three feet in diameter. And a tiny pile like that one tends to heat only for a short time and then cool off rapidly. Larger piles tend to heat much faster and remain hot long enough to allow significant decomposition to occur. Most composters consider a four foot cube to be a minimum practical size. Industrial or municipal composters build windrows up to ten feet at the base, seven feet high, and as long as they want.

However, even if you have unlimited material there is still a limit to the heap's size and that limiting factor is air supply. The bigger the compost pile the harder it becomes to get oxygen into the center. Industrial composters may have power equipment that simultaneously turns and sprays water, mechanically oxygenating and remoistening a massive windrow every few days. Even poorly-financed municipal composting systems have tractors with scoop loaders to turn their piles frequently. At home the practical limit is probably a heap six or seven feet wide at the base, initially about five feet high (it will rapidly slump a foot or so once heating begins), and as long as one has material for.

Though we might like to make our compost piles so large that maintaining sufficient airflow becomes the major problem we face, the home composter rarely has enough materials on hand to build a huge heap all at once. A single lawn mowing doesn't supply that many clippings; my own kitchen compost bucket is larger and fills faster than anyone else's I know of but still only amounts to a few gallons a week except during August when we're making jam, canning vegetables, and juicing. Garden weeds are collected a wheelbarrow at a time. Leaves are seasonal. In the East the annual vegetable garden clean-up happens after the fall frost. So almost inevitably, you will be building a heap gradually.

That's probably why most garden books illustrate compost heaps as though they were layer cakes: a base layer of brush, twigs, and coarse stuff to allow air to enter, then alternating thin layers of grass clippings, leaves, weeds, garbage, grass, weeds, garbage, and a sprinkling of soil, repeated until the heap is five feet tall. It can take months to build a compost pile this way because heating and decomposition begin before the pile is finished and it sags as it is built. I recommend several practices when gradually forming a heap.

Keep a large stack of dry, coarse vegetation next to a building pile. As kitchen garbage, grass clippings, fresh manure or other wet materials come available the can be covered with and mixed into this dry material. The wetter, greener items will rehydrate the dry vegetation and usually contain more nitrogen that balances out the higher carbon of dried grass, tall weeds, and hay.

If building the heap has taken several months, the lower central area will probably be well on its way to becoming compost and much of the pile may have already dried out by the time it is fully formed. So the best time make the first turn and remoisten a long-building pile is right after it has been completed.

Instead of picturing a layer cake, you will be better off comparing composting to making bread. Flour, yeast, water, molasses, sunflower seeds, and oil aren't layered, they're thoroughly blended and then kneaded and worked together so that the yeast can interact with the other materials and bring about a miraculous chemistry that we call dough.

Carbon to nitrogen ratio

C/N is the most important single aspect that controls both the heap's ability to heat up and the quality of the compost that results. Piles composed primarily of materials with a high ratio of carbon to nitrogen do not get very hot or stay hot long enough. Piles made from materials with too low a C/N get too hot, lose a great deal of nitrogen and may "burn out."

The compost process generally works best when the heap's starting C/N is around 25:1. If sawdust, straw, or woody hay form the bulk of the pile, it is hard to bring the C/N down enough with just grass clippings and kitchen garbage. Heaps made essentially of high C/N materials need significant additions of the most potent manures and/or highly concentrated organic nitrogen sources like seed meals or slaughterhouse concentrates. The next chapter discusses the nature and properties of materials used for composting in great detail.

I have already stressed that filling this book with tables listing so-called precise amounts of C/N for compostable materials would be foolish. Even more wasteful of energy would be the composter's attempt to compute the ratio of carbon to nitrogen resulting from any mixture of materials. For those who are interested, the sidebar provides an illustration of how that might be done.

It is far more sensible to learn from experience. Gauge the proportions of materials going into a heap by the result. If the pile gets really hot and stays that way for a few weeks before gradually cooling down then the C/N was more or less right. If, after several turnings and reheatings, the material has not thoroughly decomposed, then the initial C/N was probably too high. The words "thoroughly decomposed" mean here that there are no recognizable traces of the original materials in the heap and the compost is dark brown to black, crumbly, sweet smelling and most importantly, *when worked into soil it provokes a marked growth response, similar to fertilizer.*

If the pile did not initially heat very much or the heating stage was very brief, then the pile probably lacked nitrogen. The solution for a nitrogen-deficient pile is to turn it, simultaneously blending in more nutrient-rich materials and probably a bit of water too. After a few piles have been made novice composters will begin to get the same feel for their materials as bakers have for their flour, shortening, and yeast.

Here's a simple arithmetic problem that illustrates how to balance carbon to nitrogen.

Question: I have 100 pounds of straw with a C/N of 66:1, how much chicken manure (C/N of 8:1) do I have to add to bring the total to an average C/N of 25:1.

Answer: There is 1 pound of nitrogen already in each 66 pounds of straw, so there are already about 1.5 pounds of N in 100 pounds of straw. 100 pounds of straw compost at 25:1 would have about 4 pounds of nitrogen, so I need to add about 2.5 more pounds of N. Eight pounds of chicken manure contain 1 pound of N; 16 pounds have 2. So, if I add 32 pounds of chicken manure to 100 pounds of straw, I will have 132 pounds of material containing about 5.5 pounds of N, a C/N of 132:5.5, or about 24:1.

It is also possible to err on the opposite end of the scale and make a pile with too much nitrogen. This heap will heat very rapidly, become as hot as the microbial population can tolerate, lose moisture very quickly, and probably smell of ammonia, indicating that valuable fixed nitrogen is escaping into the atmosphere. When proteins decompose their nitrogen content is normally released as ammonia gas. Most people have smelled small piles of spring grass clippings doing this very thing. Ammonia is always created when proteins decompose in any heap at any C/N. But a properly made compost pile does not permit this valuable nitrogen source to escape.

There are other bacteria commonly found in soil that uptake ammonia gas and change it to the nitrates that plants and soil life forms need to make other proteins. These nitrification microorganisms are extremely efficient at reasonable temperatures but cannot survive the extreme high temperatures that a really hot pile can achieve. They also live only in soil. That is why it is very important to ensure that about 10 percent of a compost pile is soil and to coat the outside of a pile with a frosting of rich earth that is kept damp. One other aspect of soil helps prevent ammonia loss. Clay is capable of attracting and temporarily holding on to ammonia until it is nitrified by microorganisms. Most soils contain significant amounts of clay.

The widespread presence of clay and ammonia-fixing bacteria in all soils permits industrial farmers to inject gaseous ammonia directly into the earth where it is promptly and completely altered into nitrates. A very hot pile leaking ammonia may contain too little soil, but more likely it is also so hot that the nitrifying bacteria have been killed off. Escaping ammonia is not only an offensive nuisance, valuable fertility is being lost into the atmosphere.

Weather and season.
You can adopt a number of strategies to keep weather from chilling a compost pile. Wind both lowers temperature and dries out a pile, so if at all possible, make compost in a sheltered location. Heavy, cold rains can chill and waterlog a pile. Composting under a roof will also keep hot sun from baking moisture out of a pile in summer. Using bins or other compost structures can hold in heat that might otherwise be lost from the sides of unprotected heaps.

It is much easier to maintain a high core temperature when the weather is warm. It may not be so easy to make hot compost heaps during a northern winter. So in some parts of the country I would not expect too much from a compost pile made from autumn cleanup. This stack of leaves and frost-bitten garden plants may have to await the spring thaw, then to be mixed with potent spring grass clippings and other nitrogenous materials in order to heat up and complete the composting process. What to do with kitchen garbage during winter in the frozen

North makes an interesting problem and leads serious recyclers to take notice of vermicomposting. (See Chapter 6.)

In southern regions the heap may be prevented from overheating by making it smaller or not as tall. Chapter 9 describes in great detail how Sir Albert Howard handled the problem of high air temperature while making compost in India.

The Fertilizing Value of Compost

It is not possible for me to tell you how well your own homemade compost will fertilize plants. Like home-brewed beer and home-baked bread you can be certain that your compost may be the equal of or superior to almost any commercially made product and certainly will be better fertilizer than the high carbon result of municipal solid waste composting. But first, let's consider two semi-philosophical questions, "good for what?" and "poor as what?"

Any compost is a "social good" if it conserves energy, saves space in landfills and returns some nutrients and organic matter to the soil, whether for lawns, ornamental plantings, or vegetable gardens. Compared to the fertilizer you would have purchased in its place, any homemade compost will be a financial gain unless you buy expensive motor-powered grinding equipment to produce only small quantities.

Making compost is also a "personal good." For a few hours a year, composting gets you outside with a manure fork in your hand, working up a sweat. You intentionally participate in a natural cycle: the endless rotation of carbon from air to organic matter in the form of plants, to animals, and finally all of it back into soil. You can observe the miraculous increase in plant and soil health that happens when you intensify and enrich that cycle of carbon on land under your control.

So any compost is good compost. But will it be good fertilizer? Answering that question is a lot harder: it depends on so many factors. The growth response you'll get from compost depends on what went into the heap, on how much nitrate nitrogen was lost as ammonia during decomposition, on how completely decomposition was allowed to proceed, and how much nitrate nitrogen was created by microbes during ripening.

The growth response from compost also depends on the soil's temperature. Just like every other biological process, the nutrients in compost only GROW the plant when they decompose in the soil and are released. Where summer is hot, where the average of day and night temperatures are high, where soil temperatures reach 80° for much of the frost-free season, organic matter rots really fast and a little compost of average quality makes a huge increase in plant growth. Where summer is cool and soil organic matter decomposes slowly, poorer grades of compost have little immediate effect, or worse, may temporarily interfere with plant growth. Hotter soils are probably more desperate for organic matter and may give you a marked growth response from even poor quality compost; soils in cool climates naturally contain higher quantities of humus and need to be stoked with more potent materials if high levels of nutrients are to be released.

Compost is also reputed to make enormous improvements in the workability, or tilth of the soil. This aspect of gardening is so important and so widely misunderstood, especially by organic gardeners, that most of Chapter 7 is devoted to considering the roles of humus in the soil.

One of the things I enjoy most while gardening is GROWing some of my plants. I don't GROW them all because there is no point in having giant parsley or making the corn patch get one foot taller. Making everything get as large as possible wouldn't result in maximum nutrition either. But just for fun, how about a 100-plus pound pumpkin? A twenty-pound savoy cabbage? A cauliflower sixteen inches in diameter? An eight-inch diameter beet? Now that's GROWing!

Here's how. Simply remove as many growth limiters as possible and watch the plant's own efforts take over. One of the best examples I've ever seen of how this works was in a neighbor's backyard greenhouse. This retired welder liked his liquor. Having more time than money and little respect for legal absurdities, he had constructed a small stainless steel pot still, fermented his own mash, and made a harsh, hangover-producing whiskey from grain and cane sugar that

Appalachians call "popskull." To encourage rapid fermentation, his mashing barrel was kept in the warm greenhouse. The bubbling brew gave off large quantities of carbon dioxide gas.

The rest of his greenhouse was filled with green herbs that flowered fragrantly in September. Most of them were four or five feet tall but those plants on the end housing the mash barrel were seven feet tall and twice as bushy. Why? Because the normal level of atmospheric CO_2 actually limits plant growth.

We can't increase the carbon supply outdoors. But we can loosen the soil eighteen to twenty-four inches down (or more for deeply-rooting species) in an area as large as the plant's root system could possibly ramify during its entire growing season. I've seen some GROWers dig holes four feet deep and five feet in diameter for individual plants. We can use well-finished, strong compost to increase the humus content of that soil, and supplement that with manure tea or liquid fertilizer to provide all the nutrients the plant could possibly use. We can allocate only one plant to that space and make sure absolutely no competition develops in that space for light, water, or nutrients. We can keep the soil moist at all times. By locating the plant against a reflective white wall we can increase its light levels and perhaps the nighttime temperatures (plants make food during the day and use it to grow with at night).

Textural improvements from compost depend greatly on soil type. Sandy and loamy soils naturally remain open and workable and sustain good tilth with surprisingly small amounts of organic matter. Two or three hundred pounds (dry weight) of compost per thousand square feet per year will keep coarse-textured soils in wonderful physical condition. This small amount of humus is also sufficient to encourage the development of a lush soil ecology that creates the natural health of plants.

Silty soils, especially ones with more clay content, tend to become compacted and when low in humus will crust over and puddle when it rains hard. These may need a little more compost, perhaps in the range of three to five hundred pounds per thousand square feet per year.

Clay soils on the other hand are heavy and airless, easily compacted, hard to work, and hard to keep workable. The mechanical properties of clay soils greatly benefit from additions of organic matter several times larger than what soils composed of larger particles need. Given adequate organic matter, even a heavy clay can be made to behave somewhat like a rich loam does.

Perhaps you've noticed that I've still avoided answering the question, "how good is your compost?" First, lets take a look at laboratory analyses of various kinds of compost, connect that to what they were made from and that to the kind of growing results one might get from them. I apologize that despite considerable research I was unable to discover more detailed breakdowns from more composting activities. But the data I do have is sufficient to appreciate the range of possibilities.

Considered as a fertilizer to GROW plants, Municipal Solid Waste (MSW) compost is the lowest grade material I know of. It is usually broadcast as a surface mulch. The ingredients municipal composters must process include an indiscriminate mixture of all sorts of urban organic waste: paper, kitchen garbage, leaves, chipped tree trimmings, commercial organic garbage like restaurant waste, cannery wastes, etc. Unfortunately, paper comprises the largest single ingredient and it is by nature highly resistant to decomposition. MSW composting is essentially a recycling process, so no soil, no manure and no special low C/N sources are used to improve the fertilizing value of the finished product.

Municipal composting schemes usually must process huge volumes of material on very valuable land close to cities. Economics mean the heaps are made as large as possible, run as fast as possible, and gotten off the field without concern for developing their highest qualities. Since it takes a long time to reduce large proportions of carbon, especially when they are in very decomposition-resistant forms like paper, and since the use of soil in the compost heap is essential to prevent nitrate loss, municipal composts tend to be low in nitrogen and high in carbon. By comparison, the poorest home garden compost I could find test results for was about equal to the best municipal compost. The best garden sample ("B") is pretty fine stuff. I could not discover the ingredients that went into either garden compost but my supposition is that gardener "A" incorporated large quantities of high C/N materials like straw, sawdust and the like while gardener "B" used manure, fresh vegetation, grass clippings and other similar low C/N materials. The next chapter will evaluate the suitability of materials commonly used to make compost.

Analyses of Various Composts

Source	N%	P%	K%	Ca%	C/N
Vegetable trimmings & paper	1.57	0.40	0.40		24:1
Municipal refuse	0.97	0.16	0.21		24:1
Johnson City refuse	0.91	0.22	0.91	1.91	36:1
Gainsville, FL refuse	0.57	0.26	0.22	1.88	?
Garden compost "A"	1.40	0.30	0.40		25:1
Garden compost "B"	3.50	1.00	2.00		10:1

To interpret this chart, let's make as our standard of comparison the actual gardening results from some very potent organic material I and probably many of my readers have probably used: bagged chicken manure compost. The most potent I've ever purchased is inexpensively sold in one-cubic-foot plastic sacks stacked up in front of my local supermarket every spring. The sacks are labeled 4-3-2. I've successfully grown quite a few huge, handsome, and healthy vegetables with this product. I've also tried other similar sorts also labeled "chicken manure compost" that are about half as potent.

From many years of successful use I know that 15 to 20 sacks (about 300–400 dry-weight pounds) of 4-3-2 chicken compost spread and tilled into one thousand square feet will grow a magnificent garden. Most certainly a similar amount of the high analysis Garden "B" compost would do about the same job. Would three times as much less potent compost from Garden "A" or five times as much even poorer stuff from the Johnson City municipal composting operation do as well? Not at all! Neither would three times as many sacks of dried steer manure. Here's why.

If composted organic matter is spread like mulch atop the ground on lawns or around ornamentals and allowed to remain there its nitrogen content and C/N are not especially important. Even if the C/N is still high soil animals will continue the job of decomposition much as happens on the forest floor. Eventually their excrement will be transported into the soil by earthworms. By that time the C/N will equal that of other soil humus and no disruption will occur to the soil's process.

Growing vegetables is much more demanding than growing most perennial ornamentals or lawns. Excuse me, flower gardeners, but I've observed that even most flowers will thrive if only slight improvements are made in their soil. The same is true for most herbs. Difficulties with ornamentals or herbs are usually caused by attempting to grow a species that is not particularly well-adapted to the site or climate. Fertilized with sacked steer manure or mulched with average-to-poor compost, most ornamentals will grow adequately.

But vegetables are delicate, pampered critters that must grow as rapidly as they can grow if they are to be succulent, tasty, and yield heavily. Most of them demand very high levels of available nutrients as well as soft, friable soil containing reasonable levels of organic matter. So it is extremely important that a vegetable gardener understand the inevitable disruption occurring when organic matter that has a C/N is much above 12:1 is tilled into soil.

Organic matter that has been in soil for a while has been altered into a much studied substance, humus. We know for example that humus always has a carbon to nitrogen ratio of from 10:1 to about 12:1, just like compost from Garden "B." Garden writers call great compost like this, "stable humus," because it is slow to decompose. Its presence in soil steadily feeds a healthy ecology of microorganisms important to plant health, and whose activity accelerates release of plant nutrients from undecomposed rock particles. Humus is also fertilizer because its gradual decomposition provides mineral nutrients that make plants grow. The most important of these nutrients is nitrate nitrogen, thus soil scientists may call humus decomposition "nitrification."

When organic material with a C/N below 12:1 is mixed into soil its breakdown is very rapid. Because it contains more nitrogen than stable humus does, nitrogen is rapidly released to feed the plants and soil life. Along with nitrogen comes other plant nutrients. This accelerated nitrification continues until the remaining nitrogen balances with the remaining carbon at a ratio of about 12:1. Then the soil returns to equilibrium. The lower the C/N the more rapid the release, and the more violent the reaction in the soil. Most low C/N organic materials, like seed meal or chicken manure, rapidly release nutrients for a month or two before stabilizing. What has been described here is fertilizer.

When organic material with a C/N higher than 12:1 is tilled into soil, soil animals and microorganisms find themselves with an unsurpassed carbohydrate banquet. Just as in a compost heap, within days bacteria and fungi can multiply to match any food supply. But to construct their bodies these microorganisms need the same nutrients that plants need to grow—nitrogen, potassium, phosphorus, calcium, magnesium, etc. There are never enough of these nutrients in high C/N organic matter to match the needs of soil bacteria, especially never enough nitrogen, so soil microorganisms uptake these nutrients from the soil's reserves while they "bloom" and rapidly consume all the new carbon presented to them.

During this period of rapid decomposition the soil is thoroughly robbed of plant nutrients. And nitrification stops. Initially, a great deal of carbon dioxide gas may be given off, as carbon is metabolically "burned." However, CO_2 in high concentrations can be toxic to sprouting seeds and consequently, germination failures may occur. When I was in the seed business I'd get a few complaints every year from irate gardeners demanding to know why every seed packet they sowed failed to come up well. There were two usual causes. Either before sowing all the seeds were exposed to temperatures above 110° or more likely, a large quantity of high C/N "manure" was tilled into the garden just before sowing. In soil so disturbed transplants may also fail to grow for awhile. If the "manure" contains a large quantity of sawdust the soil will seem very infertile for a month or three.

Sir Albert Howard had a unique and pithy way of expressing this reality. He said that soil was not capable of working two jobs at once. You could not expect it to nitrify humus while it was also being required to digest organic matter. That's one reason he thought composting was such a valuable process. The digestion of organic matter proceeds outside the soil; when finished product, humus, is ready for nitrification, it is tilled in.

Rapid consumption of carbon continues until the C/N of the new material drops to the range of stable humus. Then decay microorganisms die off and the nutrients they hoarded are released back into the soil. How long the soil remains inhospitable to plant growth and seed germination depends on soil temperature, the amount of the material and how high its C/N is, and the amount of nutrients the soil is holding in reserve. The warmer and more fertile the soil was before the addition of high C/N organic matter, the faster it will decompose.

Judging by the compost analyses in the table, I can see why some municipalities are having difficulty disposing of the solid waste compost they are making. One governmental composting operation that does succeed in selling everything they can produce is Lane County, Oregon. Their *yard waste compost* is eagerly paid for by local gardeners. Lane County compost is made only from autumn leaves, grass clippings, and other yard wastes. No paper!

Yard waste compost is a product much like a homeowner would produce. And yard waste compost contains no industrial waste or any material that might pose health threats. All woody materials are finely chipped before composting and comprise no more than 20 percent of the total undecayed mass by weight. Although no nutrient analysis has been done by the county other than testing for pH (around 7.0) and, because of the use of weed and feed fertilizers on lawns, for 2-4D (no residual trace ever found present), I estimate that the overall C/N of the materials going into the windrows at 25:1. I wouldn't be surprised if the finished compost has a C/N close to 12:1.

Incidentally, Lane County understands that many gardeners don't have pickup trucks. They reasonably offer to deliver their compost for a small fee if at least one yard is purchased. Other local governments also make and deliver yard waste compost.

So what about your own home compost? If you are a flower, ornamental, or lawn grower, you have nothing to worry about. Just compost everything you have available and use all you wish to make. If tilling your compost into soil seems to slow the growth of plants, then mulch with it and avoid tilling it in, or adjust the C/N down by adding fertilizers like seed meal when tilling it in.

If you are a vegetable gardener and your compost doesn't seem to provoke the kind of growth response you hoped for, either shallowly till in compost in the fall for next year's planting, by which time it will have become stable humus, or read further. The second half of this book contains numerous hints about how to make potent compost and about how to use complete organic fertilizers in combination with compost to grow the lushest garden imaginable.

Chapter 4

All About Materials

In most parts of the country, enough organic materials accumulate around an average home and yard to make all the compost a backyard garden needs. You probably have weeds, leaves, perhaps your own human hair (my wife is the family barber), dust from the vacuum cleaner, kitchen garbage and grass clippings. But, there may not be enough to simultaneously build the lushest lawn, the healthiest ornamentals *and* grow the vegetables. If you want to make more compost than your own land allows, it is not difficult to find very large quantities of organic materials that are free or cost very little.

The most obvious material to bring in for composting is animal manure. Chicken and egg raisers and boarding stables often give manure away or sell it for a nominal fee. For a few dollars most small scale animal growers will cheerfully use their scoop loader to fill your pickup truck till the springs sag.

As useful as animal manure can be in a compost pile, there are other types of low C/N materials too. Enormous quantities of loose alfalfa accumulate around hay bale stacks at feed and grain stores. To the proprietor this dusty chaff is a nuisance gladly given to anyone that will neatly sweep it up and truck it away. To the home gardener, alfalfa in any form is rich as gold.

Some years, rainy Oregon weather is still unsettled at haying season and farmers are stuck with spoiled hay. I'm sure this happens most places that grass hay is grown on natural rainfall. Though a shrewd farmer may try to sell moldy hay at a steep discount by representing it to still have feed value, actually these ruined bales must be removed from a field before they interfere with working the land. A hard bargainer can often get spoiled hay in exchange for hauling the wet bales out of the field.

There's one local farmer near me whose entire family tree holds a well-deserved reputation for hard, self-interested dealing. One particularly wet, cool, unsettled haying season, after starting the spoiled-hay dicker at 90 cents per bale asked—nothing offered but hauling the soggy bales out of the field my offer—I finally agreed to take away about twenty tons at ten cents per bale. This small sum allowed the greedy b——d to feel he had gotten the better of me. He needed that feeling far more than I needed to win the argument or to keep the few dollars. Besides, the workings of self-applied justice that some religious philosophers call karma show that over the long haul the worst thing one person can do to another is to allow the other to get away with an evil act.

Any dedicated composter can make contacts yielding cheap or free organic materials by the ton. Orchards may have badly bruised or rotting fruit. Small cider mills, wineries, or a local juice bar restaurant may be glad to get rid of pomace. Carpentry shops have sawdust. Coffee roasters have dust and chaff. The microbrewery is becoming very popular these days; mall-scale local brewers and distillers may have spent hops and mash. Spoiled product or chaff may be available from cereal mills.

City governments often will deliver autumn leaves by the ton and will give away or sell the output of their own municipal composting operations. Supermarkets, produce wholesalers, and restaurants may be willing to give away boxes of trimmings and spoiled food. Barbers and poodle groomers throw away hair.

Seafood processors will sell truckloads of fresh crab, fish and shrimp waste for a small fee. Of course, this material becomes evil-smelling in very short order but might be relatively inoffensive if a person had a lot of spoiled hay or sawdust waiting to mix into it. Market gardeners near the Oregon coast sheet-compost crab waste, tilling it into the soil before it gets too "high." Other parts of the country might supply citrus wastes, sugar cane bagasse, rice hulls, etc.

About Common Materials

Alfalfa is a protein-rich perennial legume mainly grown as animal feed. On favorable soil it develops a deep root system, sometimes exceeding ten feet. Alfalfa draws heavily on subsoil minerals so it will be as rich or poor in nutrients as the subsoil it grew in. Its average C/N is around 12:1 making alfalfa useful to compensate for larger quantities of less potent material. Sacked alfalfa meal or pellets are usually less expensive (and being "stemmy," have a slightly higher C/N) than leafy, best-quality baled alfalfa hay. Rain-spoiled bales of alfalfa hay are worthless as animal feed but far from valueless to the composter.

Pelletized rabbit feed is largely alfalfa fortified with grain. Naturally, rabbit manure has a C/N very similar to alfalfa and is nutrient rich, especially if some provision is made to absorb the urine.

Apple pomace is wet and compact. If not well mixed with stiff, absorbent material, large clumps of this or other fruit wastes can become airless regions of anaerobic decomposition. Having a high water content can be looked upon as an advantage. Dry hay and sawdust can be hard to moisten thoroughly; these hydrate rapidly when mixed with fruit pulp. Fermenting fruit pulp attracts yellow jackets so it is sensible to incorporate it quickly into a pile and cover well with vegetation or soil.

The watery pulp of fruits is not particularly rich in nutrients but apple, grape, and pear pulps are generously endowed with soft, decomposable seeds. Most seeds contain large quantities of phosphorus, nitrogen, and other plant nutrients. It is generally true that plants locate much of their entire yearly nutrient assimilation into their seeds to provide the next generation with the best possible start. Animals fed on seeds (such as chickens) produce the richest manures.

Older books about composting warn about metallic pesticide residues adhering to fruit skins. However, it has been nearly half a century since arsenic and lead arsenate were used as pesticides and mercury is no longer used in fungicides.

Bagasse is the voluminous waste product from extracting cane sugar. Its C/N is extremely high, similar to wheat straw or sawdust, and it contains very little in the way of plant nutrients. However, its coarse, strong, fibrous structure helps build lightness into a pile and improve air flow. Most sugar mills burn bagasse as their heat source to evaporate water out of the sugary juice squeezed from the canes. At one time there was far more bagasse produced than the mills needed to burn and bagasse often became an environmental pollutant. Then, bagasse was available for nothing or next to nothing. These days, larger, modern mills generate electricity with bagasse and sell their surplus to the local power grid. Bagasse is also used to make construction fiberboard for subwall and insulation.

Banana skins and stalks are soft and lack strong fiber. They are moderately rich in phosphorus, potassium, and nitrogen. Consequently they rot quickly. Like other kitchen garbage, banana waste should be put into the core of a compost pile to avoid attracting and breeding flies. See also: *Garbage.*

Basic slag is an industrial waste from smelting iron. Ore is refined by heating it with limestone and dolomite. The impurities combine with calcium and magnesium, rise to the surface of the molten metal, and are skimmed off. Basic slag contains quite a bit of calcium plus a variety of useful plant nutrients not usually found in limestone. Its exact composition varies greatly depending on the type of ore used.

Slag is pulverized and sold in sacks as a substitute for agricultural lime. The intense biological activity of a compost pile releases more of slag's other mineral content and converts its nutrients to organic substances that become rapidly available once the compost is incorporated into soil. Other forms of powdered mineralized rock can be similarly added to a compost pile to accelerate nutrient release.

Rodale Press, publisher of *Organic Gardening* magazine, is located in Pennsylvania where steel mills abound. Having more experience with slag, Rodale advises the user to be alert to the fact that some contain little in the way of useful nutrients and/or may contain excessive amounts of sulfur. Large quantities of sulfur can acidify soil. Read the analysis on the label. Agriculturally useful slag has an average composition of 40 percent calcium and 5 percent magnesium. It must also be very finely ground to be effective. See also: *Lime* and *Rock dust.*

Beet wastes, like bagasse, are a residue of extracting sugar. They have commercial value as livestock feed and are sold as dry pulp in feed stores located near regions where sugar beets are grown. Their C/N is in the vicinity of 20:1 and they may contain high levels of potassium, reaching as much as 4 percent.

Brewery wastes. Both spent hops (dried flowers and leaves) and malt (sprouted barley and often other grains) are potent nutrient sources with low C/N ratios. Spent malt is especially potent because brewers extract all the starches and convert them to sugar, but consider the proteins as waste because proteins in the brew make it cloudy and opaque. Hops may be easier to get. Malt has uses as animal feed and may be contracted for by some local feedlot or farmer. These materials will be wet, heavy and fruitily odoriferous (though not unpleasantly so) and you will want to incorporate them into your compost pile immediately.

Buckwheat hulls. Buckwheat is a grain grown in the northeastern United States and Canada. Adapted to poor, droughty soils, the crop is often grown as a green manure. The seeds are enclosed in a thin-walled, brown to black fibrous hulls that are removed at a groat mill. Buckwheat hulls are light, springy, and airy. They'll help fluff up a compost heap. Buckwheat hulls are popular as a mulch because they adsorb moisture easily, look attractive, and stay in place. Their C/N is high. Oat and rice hulls are similar products.

Canola meal. See: *Cottonseed meal.*

Castor pomace is pulp left after castor oil has been squeezed from castor bean seeds. Like other oil seed residues it is very high in nitrogen, rich in other plant nutrients, particularly phosphorus, Castor pomace may be available in the deep South; it makes a fine substitute for animal manure.

Citrus wastes may be available to gardeners living near industrial processors of orange, lemon, and grapefruit. In those regions, dried citrus pulp may also be available in feed stores. Dried orange skins contain about 3 percent phosphorus and 27 percent potassium. Lemons are a little higher in phosphorus but lower in potassium. Fruit culls would have a similar nutrient ratio on a dry weight basis, but they are largely water. Large quantities of culls could be useful to hydrate stubbornly dry materials like straw or sawdust.

Like other by-products of industrial farming, citrus wastes may contain significant amounts of pesticide residues. The composting process will break down and eliminate most toxic organic residues, especially if the pile gets really hot through and through. (See also: *Leaves)* The effect of such high levels of potassium on the nutritional qualities of my food would also concern me if the compost I was making from these wastes were used for vegetable gardening.

Coffee grounds are nutrient-rich like other seed meals. Even after brewing they can contain up to 2 percent nitrogen, about 1/2% phosphorus and varying amounts of potassium usually well below 1 percent. Its C/N runs around 12:1. Coffee roasters and packers need to dispose of coffee chaff, similar in nutrient value to used grounds and may occasionally have a load of overly roasted beans.

Coffee grounds seem the earthworm's food of choice. In worm bins, used grounds are more vigorously devoured than any other substance. If slight odor is a consideration, especially if doing in-the-home vermicomposting, coffee grounds should be incorporated promptly into a pile to avoid the souring that results from vinegar-producing bacteria. Fermenting grounds may also attract harmless fruit flies. Paper filters used to make drip coffee may be put into the heap or worm box where they contribute to the bedding. See also: *Paper.*

Corncobs are no longer available as an agricultural waste product because modern harvesting equipment shreds them and spits the residue right back into the field. However, home gardeners who fancy sweet corn may produce large quantities of cobs. Whole cobs will aerate compost heaps but are slow to decompose. If you want your pile ready within one year, it is better to dry and then grind the cobs before composting them.

Cottonseed meal is one of this country's major oil seed residues. The seed is ginned out of the cotton fiber, ground, and then its oil content is chemically extracted. The residue, sometimes called oil cake or seed cake, is very high in protein and rich in NPK. Its C/N runs around 5:1, making it an excellent way to balance a compost pile containing a lot of carboniferous materials.

Most cottonseed meal is used as animal feed, especially for beef and dairy cattle. Purchased in garden stores in small containers it is very expensive; bought by the 50- to 80-pound sack from feed stores or farm coops, cottonseed meal and other oil seed meals are quite inexpensive. Though prices of these types of commodities vary from year to year, oil cakes of all kinds usually cost between $200 to $400 per ton and only slightly higher purchased sacked in less than ton lots.

The price of any seed meal is strongly influenced by freight costs. Cottonseed meal is cheapest in the south and the southwest where cotton is widely grown. Soybean meal may be more available and priced better in the midwest. Canadian gardeners are discovering canola meal, a by-product from producing canola (or rapeseed) oil. When I took a sabbatical in Fiji, I advised local gardeners to use coconut meal, an inexpensive "waste" from extracting coconut oil. And I would not be at all surprised to discover gardeners in South Dakota using sunflower meal. Sesame seed, safflower seed, peanut and oil-seed corn meals may also be available in certain localities.

Seed meals make an ideal starting point for compounding complete organic fertilizer mixes. The average NPK analysis of most seed meals is around 6-4-2. Considered as a fertilizer, oil cakes are somewhat lacking in phosphorus and sometimes in trace minerals. By supplementing them with materials like bone meal, phosphate rock, kelp meal, sometimes potassium-rich rock dusts and lime or gypsum, a single, wide-spectrum slow-release trace-mineral-rich organic fertilizer source can be blended at home having an analysis of about 5-5-5. Cottonseed meal is particularly excellent for this purpose because it is a dry, flowing, odorless material that stores well. I suspect that cottonseed meal from the southwest may be better endowed with trace minerals than that from leached-out southeastern soils or soy meal from depleted midwestern farms. See the last section of Chapter 8.

Some organic certification bureaucracies foolishly prohibit or discourage the use of cottonseed meal as a fertilizer. The rationale behind this rigid self-righteousness is that cotton, being a non-food crop, is sprayed with heavy applications of pesticides and/or herbicides that are so hazardous that they not permitted on food crops. These chemicals are usually dissolved in an emulsified oil-based carrier and the cotton plant naturally concentrates pesticide residues and breakdown products into the oily seed.

I believe that this concern is accurate as far as pesticide residues being translocated into the seed. However, the chemical process used to extract cottonseed oil is very efficient The ground seeds are mixed with a volatile solvent similar to ether and heated under pressure in giant retorts. I reason that when the solvent is squeezed from the seed, it takes with it all not only the oil, but, I believe, virtually all of the pesticide residues. Besides, any remaining organic toxins will be further destroyed by the biological activity of the soil and especially by the intense heat of a compost pile.

What I *personally* worry about is cottonseed oil. I avoid prepared salad dressings that may contain cottonseed oil, as well as many types of corn and potato chips, tinned oysters, and other prepared food products. I also suggest that you peek into the back of your favorite Oriental and fast food restaurants and see if there aren't stacks of ten gallon cottonseed oil cans waiting to fill the deep-fat fryer. I fear this sort of meal as dangerous to my health. If you still fear that cottonseed meal is also a dangerous product then you certainly won't want to be eating feedlot beef or drinking milk or using other dairy products from cattle fed on cottonseed meal.

Blood meal runs 10–12 percent nitrogen and contains significant amounts of phosphorus. It is the only organic fertilizer that is naturally water soluble. Blood meal, like other slaughterhouse wastes, may be too expensive for use as a compost activator.

Sprinkled atop soil as a side-dressing, dried blood usually provokes a powerful and immediate growth response. Blood meal is so potent that it is capable of burning plants; when applied you must avoid getting it on leaves or stems. Although principally a source of nitrogen, I reason that there are other nutritional substances like growth hormones or complex organic "phytamins" in blood meal. British glasshouse lettuce growers widely agree that lettuce side dressed with blood meal about three weeks before harvest has a better "finish," a much longer shelf-life, and a reduced tendency to "brown butt" compared to lettuce similarly fertilized with urea or chemical nitrate sources.

Feathers are the birds' equivalent of hair on animals and have similar properties. See *Hair*.

Fish and shellfish waste. These proteinaceous, high-nitrogen and trace-mineral-rich materials are readily available at little or no cost in pickup load lots from canneries and sea food processors. However, in compost piles, large quantities of these materials readily putrefy, make the pile go anaerobic, emit horrid odors, and worse, attract vermin and flies. To avoid these problems, fresh seafood wastes must be immediately mixed with large quantities of dry, high C/N material. There probably are only a few homestead composters able to utilize a ton or two of wet fish waste at one time.

Oregonians pride themselves for being tolerant, slow-to-take-offense neighbors. Along the Oregon coast, small-scale market gardeners will thinly spread shrimp or crab waste atop a field and promptly till it in. Once incorporated in the soil, the odor rapidly dissipates. In less than one week.

Fish meal is a much better alternative for use around the home. Of course, you have to have no concern for cost and have your mind fixed only on using the finest possible materials to produce the nutritionally finest food when electing to substitute fish meal for animal manures or oil cakes. Fish meal is much more potent than cottonseed meal. Its typical nutrient analysis runs 9-6-4. However, figured per pound of nutrients they contain, seed meals are a much less expensive way to buy NPK. Fish meal is also mildly odoriferous. The smell is nothing like wet seafood waste, but it can attract cats, dogs, and vermin.

What may make fish meal worth the trouble and expense is that sea water is the ultimate depository of all water-soluble nutrients that were once in the soil. Animals and plants living in the sea enjoy complete, balanced nutrition. Weston Price's classic book, *Nutrition and Physical Degeneration,* attributes nearly perfect health to humans who made seafoods a significant portion of their diets. Back in the 1930s—before processed foods were universally available in the most remote locations- people living on isolated sea coasts tended to live long, have magnificent health, and perfect teeth. See also: *Kelp meal.*

Garbage. Most forms of kitchen waste make excellent compost. But Americans foolishly send megatons of kitchen garbage to landfills or overburden sewage treatment plants by grinding garbage in a disposal. The average C/N of garbage is rather low so its presence in a compost heap facilitates the decomposition of less potent materials. Kitchen garbage can also be recycled in other ways such as vermicomposting (worm boxes) and burying it in the garden in trenches or post holes. These alternative composting methods will be discussed in some detail later.

Putting food scraps and wastes down a disposal is obviously the least troublesome and apparently the most "sanitary" method, passing the problem on to others. Handled with a little forethought, composting home food waste will not breed flies or make the kitchen untidy or ill smelling. The most important single step in keeping the kitchen clean and free of odor is to put wastes in a small plastic bucket or other container of one to two gallons in size, and empty it every few days. Periodically adding a thin layer of sawdust or peat moss supposedly helps to prevent smells. In our kitchen, we've found that covering the compost bucket is no alternative to emptying it. When incorporating kitchen wastes into a compost pile, spread them thinly and cover with an inch or two of leaves, dry grass, or hay to adsorb wetness and prevent access by flies. It may be advisable to use a vermin-tight composting bin.

Granite dust. See *Rock dust.*

Grape wastes. See *Apple pomace.*

Grass clippings. Along with kitchen garbage, grass clippings are the compostable material most available to the average homeowner. Even if you (wisely) don't compost all of your clippings (see sidebar), your foolish neighbors may bag theirs up for you to take away. If you mulch with grass clippings, make sure the neighbors aren't using "weed and feed" type fertilizers, or the clippings may cause the plants that are mulched to die. Traces of the those types of broadleaf herbicides allowed in "weed and feed" fertilizers, are thoroughly decomposed in the composting process.

It is not necessary to return every bit of organic matter to maintain a healthy lawn. Perhaps one-third to one-half the annual biomass production may be taken away and used for composting without seriously depleting the lawn's vigor—especially if one application of a quality fertilizer is given to the lawn each year. Probably the best time of year to remove clippings is during the spring while the grass is growing most rapidly. Once a clover/grass mix is established it is less necessary to use nitrogen fertilizers. In fact, high levels of soil nitrates reduces the clover's ability to fix atmospheric nitrogen. However, additions of other mineral nutrients like phosphorus, potassium, and especially calcium may still be necessary.

Lawn health is similar to garden health. Both depend on the presence of large enough quantities of organic material in the soil. This organic matter holds a massive reserve of nutrition built up over the years by the growing plants themselves. When, for reasons of momentary aesthetics, we bag up and remove clippings from our lawn, we prevent the grass from recycling its own fertility.

It was once mistakenly believed that unraked lawn clippings built up on the ground as unrotted thatch, promoting harmful insects and diseases. This is a half truth. Lawns repeatedly fertilized with sulfur-based chemical fertilizers, especially ammonium sulfate and superphosphate, become so acid and thus so hostile to bacterial decomposition and soil animals that a thatch of unrotted clippings and dead sod can build up and thus promote disease and insect problems.

However, lawns given lime or gypsum to supply calcium that is so vital to the healthy growth of clover, and seed meals and/or dressings of finely decomposed compost or manure become naturally healthy. Clippings falling on such a lawn rot rapidly because of the high level of microorganisms in the soil, and disappear in days. Dwarf white clover can produce all the nitrate nitrogen that grasses need to stay green and grow lustily. Once this state of health is developed, broadleaf weeds have a hard time competing with the lusty grass/clover sod and gradually disappear. Fertilizing will rarely be necessary again if little biomass is removed.

Homeowners who demand the spiffy appearance of a raked lawn but still want a healthy lawn have several options. They may compost their grass clippings and then return the compost to the lawn. They may use a side-discharge mower and cut two days in succession. The first cut will leave rows of clippings to dry on the lawn; the second cut will disintegrate those clippings and pretty much make them disappear. Finally, there are "mulching" mowers with blades that chop green grass clippings into tiny pieces and drops them below the mower where they are unnoticeable.

Grass clippings, especially spring grass, are very high in nitrogen, similar to the best horse or cow manure. Anyone who has piled up fresh grass clippings has noticed how rapidly they heat up, how quickly the pile turns into a slimy, airless, foul-smelling anaerobic mess, and how much ammonia may be given off. Green grass should be thoroughly dispersed into a pile, with plenty of dry material. Reserve bags of leaves from the fall or have a bale of straw handy to mix in if needed. Clippings allowed to sun dry for a few days before raking or bagging behave much better in the compost heap.

Greensand. See *Rock dust.*

Hair contains ten times the nitrogen of most manures. It resists absorbing moisture and readily compresses, mats, and sheds water, so hair needs to be mixed with other wetter materials. If I had easy access to a barber shop, beauty salon, or poodle grooming business, I'd definitely use hair in my compost. Feathers, feather meal and feather dust (a bird's equivalent to hair) have similar qualities.

Hay. In temperate climates, pasture grasses go through an annual cycle that greatly changes their nutrient content. Lawn grasses are not very different. The first cuttings of spring grass are potent sources of nitrogen, high in protein and other vital mineral nutrients. In fact, spring grass may be as good an animal feed as alfalfa or other legume hay. Young ryegrass, for example, may exceed two percent nitrogen-equaling about 13 percent protein. That's why cattle and horses on fresh spring grass frisk around and why June butter is so dark yellow, vitamin-rich and good-flavored.

In late spring, grasses begin to form seed and their chemical composition changes. With the emergence of the seed stalk, nitrogen content drops markedly and the leaves become more fibrous, ligneous, and consequently, more reluctant to decompose. At pollination ryegrass has dropped to about 1 percent nitrogen and by the time mature seed has developed, to about 0.75 percent.

These realities have profound implications for hay-making, for using grasses as green manures, and for evaluating the C/N of hay you may be planning to use in a compost heap. In earlier times, making grass hay that would be nutritious enough to maintain the health of cattle required cutting the grass before, or just at, the first appearance of seed stalks. Not only did early harvesting greatly reduce the bulk yield, it usually meant that without concern for cost or hours of labor the grass had to be painstakingly dried at a time of year when there were more frequent rains and lower temperatures. In nineteenth-century England, drying grass was draped by hand over low hurdles, dotting each pasture with hundreds of small racks that shed water like thatched roofs and allowed air flow from below. It is obvious to me where the sport of running hurdles came from; I envision energetic young country folk, pepped up on that rich spring milk and the first garden greens of the year, exuberantly racing each other across the just-mowed fields during haying season.

In more recent years, fresh wet spring grass was packed green into pits and made into silage where a controlled anaerobic fermentation retained its nutritional content much like sauerkraut keeps cabbage. Silage makes drying unnecessary. These days, farm labor is expensive and tractors are relatively inexpensive. It seems that grass hay must be cut later when the weather is more stable, economically dried on the ground, prevented from molding by frequent raking, and then baled mechanically.

In regions enjoying relatively rainless springs or where agriculture depends on irrigation, this system may result in quality hay. But most modern farmers must supplement the low-quality hay with oil cakes or other concentrates. Where I live, springs are cool and damp and the weather may not stabilize until mid-June. By this date grass seed is already formed and beginning to dry down. This means our local grass hay is very low in protein, has a high C/N, and is very woody—little better than wheat straw. Pity the poor horses and cattle that must try to extract enough nutrition from this stuff.

Western Oregon weather conditions also mean that farmers often end up with rain-spoiled hay they are happy to sell cheaply. Many years I've made huge compost piles largely from this kind of hay. One serious liability from cutting grass hay late is that it will contain viable seeds. If the composting process does not thoroughly heat all of these seeds, the compost will sprout grass all over the garden. One last difficulty with poor quality grass hay: the tough, woody stems are reluctant to absorb moisture.

The best way to simultaneously overcome all of these liabilities is first to permit the bales to thoroughly spoil and become moldy through and through before composting them. When I have a ton or two of spoiled hay bales around, I spread them out on the ground in a single layer and leave them in the rain for an entire winter. Doing this sprouts most of the grass seed within the bales, thoroughly moistens the hay, and initiates decomposition. Next summer I pick up this material, remove the baling twine, and mix it into compost piles with plenty of more nitrogenous stuff.

One last word about grass and how it works when green manuring. If a thick stand of grasses is tilled in during spring before seed formation begins, its high nitrogen content encourages rapid decomposition. Material containing 2 percent nitrogen and lacking a lot of tough fiber can be totally rotted and out of the way in two weeks, leaving the soil ready to plant. This variation on green manuring works like a charm.

However, if unsettled weather conditions prevent tillage until seed formation has begun, the grasses will contain much less nitrogen and will have developed a higher content of resistant lignins. If the soil does not become dry and large reserves of nitrogen are already waiting in the soil to balance the high C/N of mature grass, it may take only a month to decompose But there will be so much decomposition going on for the first few weeks that even seed germination is inhibited. Having to wait an unexpected month or six weeks after wet weather prevented forming an early seed bed may delay sowing for so long that the season is missed for the entire year. Obstacles like this must be kept in mind when considering using green manuring as a soil building technique. Cutting the grass close to the soil line and composting the vegetation off the field eliminates this problem.

Hoof and horn meal. Did you know that animals construct their hooves and horns from compressed hair? The meal is similar in nutrient composition to blood meal, leather dust, feather meal, or meat meal (tankage). It is a powerful source of nitrogen with significant amounts of phosphorus. Like other slaughterhouse by-products its high cost may make it impractical to use to adjust the C/N of compost piles. Seed meals or chicken manure (chickens are mainly fed seeds) have somewhat lower nitrogen contents than animal by-products but their price per pound of actual nutrition is more reasonable. If hoof and horn meal is not dispersed through a pile it may draw flies and putrefy. I would prefer to use expensive slaughterhouse concentrates to blend into organic fertilizer mixes.

Juicer pulp: See *Apple pomace.*

Kelp meals from several countries are available in feed and grain stores and better garden centers, usually in 25 kg (55-pound) sacks ranging in cost from $20 to $50. Considering this spendy price, I consider using kelp meal more justifiable in complete organic fertilizer mixes as a source of trace minerals than as a composting supplement.

There is a great deal of garden lore about kelp meal's growth-stimulating and stress-fortifying properties. Some garden-store brands tout these qualities and charge a very high price. The best prices are found at feed dealers where kelp meal is considered a bulk commodity useful as an animal food supplement.

I've purchased kelp meal from Norway, Korea, and Canada. There are probably other types from other places. I don't think there is a significant difference in the mineral content of one source compared to another. I do not deny that there may be differences in how well the packers processing method preserved kelp's multitude of beneficial complex organic chemicals that improve the growth and overall health of plants by functioning as growth stimulants, phytamins, and who knows what else.

Still, I prefer to buy by price, not by mystique, because, after gardening for over twenty years, garden writing for fifteen and being in the mail order garden seed business for seven I have been on the receiving end of countless amazing claims by touters of agricultural snake oils; after testing out dozens of such concoctions I tend to disbelieve mystic contentions of unique superiority. See also: *Seaweed*.

Leather dust is a waste product of tanneries, similar to hoof and horn meal or tankage. It may or may not be contaminated with high levels of chromium, a substance used to tan suede. If only vegetable-tanned leather is produced at the tannery in question, leather dust should be a fine soil amendment. Some organic certification bureaucrats prohibit its use, perhaps rightly so in this case.

Leaves. Soil nutrients are dissolved by rain and leached from surface layers, transported to the subsoil, thence the ground water, and ultimately into the salty sea. Trees have deep root systems, reaching far into the subsoil to bring plant nutrients back up, making them nature's nutrient recycler. Because they greatly increase soil fertility, J. Russell Smith called trees "great engines of production." Anyone who has not read his visionary book, *Tree Crops,* should. Though written in 1929, this classic book is currently in print.

Once each year, leaves are available in large quantity, but aren't the easiest material to compost. Rich in minerals but low in nitrogen, they are generally slow to decompose and tend to pack into an airless mass. However, if mixed with manure or other high-nitrogen amendment and enough firm material to prevent compaction, leaves rot as well as any other substance. Running dry leaves through a shredder or grinding them with a lawnmower greatly accelerates their decomposition. Of all the materials I've ever put through a garden grinder, dry leaves are the easiest and run the fastest.

Once chopped, leaves occupy much less volume. My neighbor, John, a very serious gardener like me, keeps several large garbage cans filled with pulverized dry leaves for use as mulch when needed. Were I a northern gardener I'd store shredded dry leaves in plastic bags over the winter to mix into compost piles when spring grass clippings and other more potent materials were available. Some people fear using urban leaves because they may contain automotive pollutants such as oil and rubber components. Such worries are probably groundless. Dave Campbell who ran the City of Portland (Oregon) Bureau of Maintenance leaf composting program said he has run tests for heavy metals and pesticide residues on every windrow of compost he has made.

Almost all our tests so far have shown less than the background level for heavy metals, and no traces of pesticides [including] chlorinated and organophosphate pesticides.... It is very rare for there to be any problem.

Campbell tells an interesting story that points out how thoroughly composting eliminates pesticide residues. He said:

Once I was curious about some leaves we were getting from a city park where I knew the trees had been sprayed with a pesticide just about a month before the leaves fell and we collected them. In this case, I had the uncomposted leaves tested and then the compost tested. In the fresh leaves a trace of ... residue was detected, but by the time the composting process was finished, no detectable level was found.

Lime. There is no disputing that calcium is a vital soil nutrient as essential to the formation of plant and animal proteins as nitrogen. Soils deficient in calcium can be inexpensively improved by adding agricultural lime which is relatively pure calcium carbonate ($CaCO_3$). The use of agricultural lime or dolomitic lime in compost piles is somewhat controversial. Even the most authoritative of authorities disagree. There is no disputing that the calcium content of plant material and animal manure resulting from that plant material is very dependent on the amount of calcium available in the soil. Chapter 8 contains quite a thorough discussion of this very phenomena. If a compost pile is made from a variety of materials grown on soils that contained adequate calcium, then adding additional lime should be unnecessary. However, if the materials being composted are themselves deficient in calcium then the organisms of decomposition may not develop fully.

While preparing this book, I queried the venerable Dr. Herbert H. Koepf about lime in the compost heap. Koepf's biodynamic books served as my own introduction to gardening in the early 1970s. He is still active though in his late seventies. Koepf believes that lime is not necessary when composting mixtures that contain significant amounts of manure because the decomposition of proteinaceous materials develops a more or less neutral pH. However, when composting mixtures of vegetation without manure, the conditions tend to become very acid and bacterial fermentation is inhibited. To correct low pH, Koepf recommends agricultural lime at 25 pounds per ton of vegetation, the weight figured on a dry matter basis. To guesstimate dry weight, remember that green vegetation is 70–80 percent water, to prevent organic material like hay from spoiling it is first dried down to below 15 percent moisture.

There is another reason to make sure that a compost pile contains an abundance of calcium. Azotobacteria, that can fix nitrate nitrogen in mellowing compost piles, depend for their activity on the availability of calcium. Adding agricultural lime in such a situation may be very useful, greatly speed the decomposition process, and improve the quality of the compost. Albert Howard used small amounts of lime in his compost piles specifically to aid nitrogen fixation. He also incorporated significant quantities of fresh bovine manure at the same time.

However, adding lime to heating manure piles results in the loss of large quantities of ammonia gas. Perhaps this is the reason some people are opposed to using lime in any composting process. Keep in mind that a manure pile is not a compost pile. Although both will heat up and decay, the starting C/N of a barnyard manure pile runs around 10:1 while a compost heap of yard waste and kitchen garbage runs 25:1 to

30:1. Any time highly nitrogenous material, such as fresh manures or spring grass clippings, are permitted to decompose without adjustment of the carbon-to-nitrogen ratio with less potent stuff, ammonia tends to be released, lime or not.

Only agricultural lime or slightly better, dolomitic lime, are useful in compost piles. Quicklime or slaked lime are made from heated limestone and undergo a violent chemical reaction when mixed with water. They may be fine for making cement, but not for most agricultural purposes.

Linseed meal. See *Cottonseed meal.*

Manure. Fresh manure can be the single most useful addition to the compost pile. What makes it special is the presence of large quantities of active digestive enzymes . These enzymes seem to contribute to more rapid heating and result in a finer-textured, more completely decomposed compost that provokes a greater growth response in plants. Manure from cattle and other multi-stomached ruminants also contains cellulose-decomposing bacteria. Soil animals supply similar digestive enzymes as they work over the litter on the forest floor but before insects and other tiny animals can eat much of a compost heap, well-made piles will heat up, driving out or killing everything except microorganisms and fungi.

All of the above might be of interest to the country dweller or serious backyard food grower but probably sounds highly impractical to most of this book's readers. Don't despair if fresh manure is not available or if using it is unappealing. Compost made with fresh, unheated manure works only a little faster and produces just a slightly better product than compost activated with seed meals, slaughterhouse concentrates, ground alfalfa, grass clippings, kitchen garbage, or even dried, sacked manures. Compost made without any manure still "makes!"

When evaluating manure keep in mind the many pitfalls. Fresh manure is very valuable, but if you obtain some that has been has been heaped up and permitted to heat up, much of its nitrogen may already have dissipated as ammonia while the valuable digestive enzymes will have been destroyed by the high temperatures at the heap's core. A similar degradation happens to digestive enzymes when manure is dried and sacked. Usually, dried manure comes from feedlots where it has also first been stacked wet and gone through a violent heating process. So if I were going to use sacked dried manure to lower the C/N of a compost pile, I'd evaluate it strictly on its cost per pound of actual nitrogen. In some cases, seed meals might be cheaper and better able to drop the heap's carbon-to-nitrogen ratio even more than manure.

There are many kinds of manure and various samples of the same type of manure may not be equal. This demonstrates the principle of what goes in comes out. Plants concentrate proteins and mineral nutrients in their seed so animals fed on seed (like chickens) excrete manure nearly as high in minerals and with a C/N like seed meals (around 8:1). Alfalfa hay is a legume with a C/N around 12:1. Rabbits fed almost exclusively on alfalfa pellets make a rich manure with a similar C/N. Spring grass and high quality hay and other leafy greens have a C/N nearly as good as alfalfa. Livestock fed the best hay supplemented with grain and silage make fairly rich manure. Pity the unfortunate livestock trying to survive as "straw burners" eating overly mature grass hay from depleted fields. Their manure will be as poor as the food and soil they are trying to live on.

When evaluating manure, also consider the nature and quantity of bedding mixed into it. Our local boarding stables keep their lazy horses on fir sawdust. The idle "riding" horses are usually fed very strawy local grass hay with just enough supplemental alfalfa and grain to maintain a minimal healthy condition. The "horse manure" I've hauled from these stables seems more sawdust than manure. It must have a C/N of 50 or 60:1 because by itself it will barely heat up.

Manure mixed with straw is usually richer stuff. Often this type comes from dairies. Modern breeds of milk cows must be fed seed meals and other concentrates to temporarily sustain them against depletion from unnaturally high milk production.

After rabbit and chicken, horse manure from well-fed animals like race horses or true, working animals may come next. Certainly it is right up there with the best cow manure. Before the era of chemical fertilizer, market gardeners on the outskirts of large cities took wagon loads of produce to market and returned with an equivalent weight of "street sweepings." What they most prized was called "short manure," or horse manure without any bedding. Manure and bedding mixtures were referred to as "long manure" and weren't considered nearly as valuable.

Finally, remember that over half the excretion of animals is urine. And far too little value is placed on urine. As early as 1900 it was well known that if you fed one ton (dry weight) of hay and measured the resulting manure after thorough drying, only 800 pounds was left. What happened to the other 1,200 pounds of dry material? Some, of course, went to grow the animal. Some was enzymatically "burned" as energy fuel and its wastes given off as CO_2 and H_2O. Most of it was excreted in liquid form. After all, what is digestion but an enzymatic conversion of dry material into a water solution so it can be circulated through the bloodstream to be used and discarded as needed. Urine also contains numerous complex organic substances and cellular breakdown products that improve the health of the soil ecology.

However, urine is not easy to capture. It tends to leach into the ground or run off when it should be absorbed into bedding. Chicken manure and the excrements of other fowl are particularly valuable in this respect because the liquids and solids of their waste are uniformly mixed so nothing is lost. When Howard worked out his system of making superior compost at Indore, he took full measure of the value of urine and paid great care to its capture and use.

Paper is almost pure cellulose and has a very high C/N like straw or sawdust. It can be considered a valuable source of bulk for composting if you're using compost as mulch. Looked upon another way, composting can be a practical way to recycle paper at home.

The key to composting paper is to shred or grind it. Layers of paper will compress into airless mats. Motor-driven hammermill shredders will make short work of dry paper. Once torn into tiny pieces and mixed with other materials, paper is no more subject to compaction than grass clippings. Even without power shredding equipment, newsprint can be shredded by hand, easily ripped into narrow strips by tearing whole sections along the grain of the paper, not fighting against it.

Evaluating Nitrogen Content

A one-cubic foot bag of dried steer manure weighs 25 pounds and is labeled 1 percent nitrogen. That means four sacks weighs 100 pounds and contains 1 pound of actual nitrogen.

A fifty pound bag of cottonseed meal contains six percent nitrogen. Two sacks weighs 100 pounds and contains 6 pounds of actual nitrogen.

Therefore it takes 24 sacks of steer manure to equal the nitrogen contained in two sacks of cottonseed meal.

If steer manure costs $1.50 per sack, six pound of actual nitrogen from steer manure costs 24 x $1.50 = $36.00.

If fifty pounds of cottonseed meal costs $7.50, then six pounds of actual nitrogen from cottonseed meal costs 2 x $7.50 = $15.00.

Now, lets take a brief moment to see why industrial farmers thinking only of immediate financial profit, use chemical fertilizers. Urea, a synthetic form of urine used as nitrogen fertilizer contains 48 percent nitrogen. So 100 pounds of urea contains 48 pounds of nitrogen. That quantity of urea also costs about $15.00! Without taking into account its value in terms of phosphorus, potassium and other mineral contents, nitrogen from seed meal costs at least eight times as much per pound as nitrogen from urea.

Newspapers, even with colored inks, can be safely used in compost piles. Though some colored inks do contain heavy metals, these are not used on newsprint.

However, before beginning to incorporate newsprint into your composting, reconsider the analyses of various types of compost broken out as a table in the previous chapter. The main reason many municipal composting programs make a low-grade product with such a high C/N is the large proportion of paper used. If your compost is intended for use as mulch around perennial beds or to be screened and broadcast atop lawns, then having a nitrogen-poor product is of little consequence. But if your compost is headed for the vegetable garden or will be used to grow the largest possible prized flowers then perhaps newsprint could be recycled in another way.

Cardboard, especially corrugated material, is superior to newsprint for compost making because its biodegradable glues contain significant amounts of nitrogen. Worms love to consume cardboard mulch. Like other forms of paper, cardboard should be shredded, ground or chopped as finely as possible, and thoroughly mixed with other materials when composted.

Pet wastes may contain disease organisms that infect humans. Though municipal composting systems can safely eliminate such diseases, home composting of dog and cat manure may be risky if the compost is intended for food gardening.

Phosphate rock. If your garden soil is deficient in phosphorus, adding rock phosphate to the compost pile may accelerate its availability in the garden, far more effectively than adding phosphate to soil. If the vegetation in your vicinity comes from soils similarly deficient in phosphorus, adding phosphate rock will support a healthier decomposition ecology and improve the quality of your compost. Five to ten pounds of rock phosphate added to a cubic yard of uncomposted organic matter is about the right amount.

Rice hulls: See *Buckwheat hulls.*

Rock dust. All plant nutrients except nitrogen originally come from decomposing rock. Not all rocks contain equal concentrations and assortments of the elements plants use for nutrients. Consequently, not all soils lustily grow healthy plants. One very natural way to improve the over all fertility of soil is to spread and till in finely ground rock flour make from highly mineralized rocks.

This method is not a new idea. Limestone and dolomite—soft, easily powdered rocks—have been used for centuries to add calcium and magnesium. For over a century, rock phosphate and kainite—a soft, readily soluble naturally occurring rock rich in potassium, magnesium and sulfur—have been ground and used as fertilizer. Other natural rock sources like Jersey greensand have long been used in the eastern United States on some unusual potassium-deficient soils.

Lately it has become fashionable to remineralize the earth with heavy applications of rock flours. Unlike most fads and trends, this one is wise and should endure. The best rocks to use are finely ground "basic" igneous rocks like basalts. They are called basic as opposed to "acid" rocks because they are richer in calcium and magnesium with lesser quantities of potassium. When soil forms from these materials it tends to not be acid. Most basic igneous rocks also contain a wide range of trace mineral nutrients. I have observed marked improvements in plant growth by incorporating ordinary basalt dust that I personally shoveled from below a conveyor belt roller at a local quarry where crushed rock was being prepared for road building. Basalt dust was an unintentional by-product.

Though highly mineralized rock dust may be a valuable soil amendment, its value must equal its cost. Application rates of one or two tons per acre are minimal. John Hamaker's *The Survival of Civilization* suggests eight to ten tons per acre the first application and then one or two tons every few years thereafter. This means the correct price for rock dust is similar to the price for agricultural lime; in my region that's about $60 to $80 a ton in sacks. Local farmers pay about $40 a ton in bulk, including spreading on your field by the seller. A fifty-pound sack of rock dust should retail for about $2. These days it probably costs several times that price, tending to keep rock dust a novelty item.

The activities of fungi and bacteria are the most potent forces making nutrients available to plants. As useful as tilling rock powders into soil may be, the intense biological activity of the compost pile accelerates their availability. And the presence of these minerals might well make a compost pile containing nutrient-deficient vegetation work faster and become better fertilizer.

Were the right types of rock dust available and cheap, I'd make it about 5 percent by volume of my heap, and equal that with rich soil.

Safflowerseed meal. See *Cottonseed meal.*

Sawdust contains virtually nothing but carbon. In small quantities it is useful to fluff up compost piles and prevent compaction. However this is only true of coarse material like that from sawmills or chain saws. The fine saw dust from carpentry and cabinet work may compact and become airless. See *Paper* for a discussion of lowering the fertilizing value of compost with high C/N materials.

Seaweed when freshly gathered is an extraordinary material for the compost pile. Like most living things from the ocean seaweeds are rich in all of the trace minerals and contain significant amounts of the major nutrients, especially potassium, with lesser amounts of phosphorus and nitrogen. Seaweeds enrich the heap, decompose very rapidly, and assist other materials to break down. Though heavy and often awkward to gather and haul, if they are available, seaweeds should not be permitted to go to waste.

Those with unlimited money may use sprinklings of kelp meal in the compost pile to get a similar effect. However, kelp meal may be more economically used as part of a complete organic fertilizer mixture that is worked into soil.

Shrub and tree prunings are difficult materials to compost unless you have a shredder/chipper. Even after being incorporated into one hot compost heap after another, half-inch diameter twigs may take several years to fully decompose. And turning a heap containing long branches can be very difficult. But buying power equipment just to grind a few cart loads of hedge and tree prunings each year may not be economical. My suggestion is to neatly tie any stick larger than your little finger into tight bundles about one foot in diameter and about 16 inches long and then burn these "faggots" in the fireplace or wood stove. This will be less work in the long run.

Soil is an often overlooked but critically important part of the compost pile. Least of its numerous benefits, soil contains infinitudes of microorganisms that help start out decomposition. Many compostable materials come with bits of soil already attached and few are sterile in themselves. But extra soil ensures that there will initially be a sufficient number and variety of these valuable organisms. Soil also contains insoluble minerals that are made soluble by biological activity. Some of these minerals may be in short supply in the organic matter itself and their addition may improve the health and vigor of the whole decomposition ecology. A generous addition of rock dust may do this even better.

Most important, soil contains nitrification microorganisms that readily convert ammonia gas to nitrates, and clay that will catch and temporarily hold ammonia. Nitrifying bacteria do not live outside of soil. Finally, a several inch thick layer of soil capping the heap serves as an extra insulator, holding in heat, raising the core temperature and helping seal in moisture. Making a compost heap as much as 10 percent soil by dry weight is the right target.

Try thinking of soil somewhat like the moderators in an atomic reactor, controlling the reaction by trapping neutrons. Soil won't change the C/N of a heap but not being subject to significant breakdown it will slightly lower the maximum temperature of decomposition; while trapping ammonia emissions; and creating better conditions for nitrogen fixing bacteria to improve the C/N as the heap cools and ripens.

Soybean meal. See *Cottonseed meal.*

Straw is a carboniferous material similar to sawdust but usually contains more nutrients. It is a valuable aerator, each stalk acting as a tube for air to enter and move through the pile. Large quantities of long straw can make it very difficult to turn a heap the first time. I'd much prefer to have manure mixed with straw than with sawdust.

Sunflowerseed meal. See *Cottonseed meal.*

Tankage is another slaughterhouse or rendering plant waste consisting of all animal refuse except blood and fat. Locally it is called meat meal. See *Hoof and horn meal.*

Tofu factory waste. Okara is the pulp left after soy milk has been squeezed from cooked, ground soybeans. Small-scale tofu makers will have many gallons of okara to dispose of each day. It makes good pig food so there may be competition to obtain it. Like any other seed waste, okara is high in nitrogen and will be wet and readily putrefiable like brewery waste. Mix into compost piles immediately.

Urine. See *Manure.*

Weeds. Their nutrient content is highly variable depending on the species and age of the plant. Weeds gone to seed are both low in nitrogen and require locating in the center of a hot heap to kill off the seeds. Tender young weeds are as rich in nitrogen as spring grass.

Weeds that propagate through underground stems or rhizomes like quack-grass, Johnsongrass, bittersweet, and the like are better burnt.

Wood ash from hardwoods is rich in potassium and contains significant amounts of calcium and other minerals. Ash from conifers may be similarly rich in potassium but contains little else. Wood ashes spread on the ground tend to lose their nutrients rapidly through leaching. If these nutrients are needed in your soil, then add the ash to your compost piles where it will become an unreachable part of the biomass that will be gradually released in the garden when the compost is used.

Wood chips are slow to decompose although they may be added to the compost pile if one is not in a hurry. Their chunkiness and stiff mechanical properties help aerate a heap. They are somewhat more nutrient rich than sawdust.

Chapter 5

Methods and Variations

Growing the majority of my family's food absorbs all of the energy I care to put into gardening. So my yard is neat but shaggy. Motivated by what I consider total rationality, my lawn is cut only when it threatens to overwhelm the lawnmower, and the lawn is not irrigated, so it browns off and stops growing in summer.

I don't grow flowers because I live on a river in a beautiful countryside setting surrounded by low mountains. Nothing I created could begin to compete with what nature freely offers my eye. One untidy bed of ornamentals by the front door are my bow to conventionality, but these fit the entrances northeast aspect by being Oregon woods natives like ferns, salal, Oregon grape and an almost wild rhododendron—all these species thrive without irrigation.

When I give lectures, I am confronted by the amazing gardening variations that humans are capable of. Some folks' raised vegetable beds are crude low mounds. Then, I am shown photographs of squared, paralleled vertical-walled raised beds, uniformly wrapped in cedar planks. Some gardens are planted in fairly straight rows, some are laid-out in carefully calculated interplanted hexagonal successions and some are a wild scattering of catch-as-catch-can. Some people don't eat many kinds of vegetables yet grow large stands of corn and beans for canning or freezing.

Others grow small patches of a great many species, creating a year-round gourmet produce stand for their personal enjoyment. Some gardeners grow English-style floral displays occupying every square inch of their yards and offering a constant succession of color and texture.

This chapter presents some of the many different ways people handle the disposal of yard and kitchen wastes. Compost making, like gardening, reflects variations in temperament. You probably weren't surprised at my casual landscaping because you already read about my unkempt compost heap. So I am similarly not surprised to discover backyard composting methods as neat as a German village, as aesthetic as a Japanese garden, as scientific as an engineer would design and as ugly as...

Containers and Other Similar Methods

In my days of youthful indiscretions I thought I could improve life on Earth by civilizing high school youth through engendering in them an understanding of history. I confess I almost completely failed and gave up teaching after a few years. However, I personally learned a great deal about history and the telling of history. I read many old journals, diaries, and travel accounts. From some of these documents I gained little while other accounts introduced me to unique individuals who assisted me in understanding their era.

It seems that what differentiates good from bad reporting is how frank and honest the reporter is about their own personal opinions, prejudices, and outlooks. The more open and direct the reporter, the better the reader can discount inevitable distortions and get a picture of what might really have been there. The more the reporter attempts to be "objective" by hiding their viewpoints, the less valuable their information.

That is why before discussing those manufactured aids to composting that can make a consumer of you, I want to inform you that I am a frugal person who shuns unnecessary expenditure. I maintain what seems to me to be a perfect justification for my stinginess: I prefer relative unemployment. Whenever I want to buy something it has become my habit first to ask myself if the desired object could possibly bring me as much pleasure as knowing that I don't have to get up and go to work the next morning. Usually I decide to save the money so I do not have to earn more. *En extremis,* I repeat the old Yankee marching chant like a mantra:

Make do! Wear it out! When it is gone, do without! Bum, Bum! Bum bi Dum! Bum bi di Dum, Bum bi Dum!

So I do not own a shredder/grinder when patience will take its place. I do not buy or make composting containers when a country life style and not conforming to the neatness standards of others makes bins or tumblers unnecessary. However, I do grudgingly accept that others live differently. Let me warn you that my descriptions of composting aids and accessories are probably a little jaundiced. I am doing my best to be fair.

Visual appeal is the primary benefit of making compost in a container. To a tidy, northern European sense of order, any composting structure will be far neater than the raw beauty of a naked heap. Composting container designs may offer additional advantages but no single structure will do everything possible. With an enclosure, it may be possible to heat up a pile smaller than 1' x 4' x 4' because the walls and sometimes the top of the container may be insulating. This is a great advantage to someone with a postage stamp backyard that treasures every square foot. Similarly, wrapping the heap retards moisture loss. Some structures shut out vermin.

On the other hand, structures can make it more difficult to make compost. Using a prefabricated bin can prevent a person from readily turning the heap and can almost force a person to also buy some sort of shredder/chipper to first reduce the size of the material. Also, viewed as a depreciating economic asset with a limited life span, many composting aids cost as much or more money as the value of all the material they can ever turn out. Financial cost relates to ecological cost, so spending money on short-lived plastic or easily rusted metal may negate any environmental benefit gained from recycling yard wastes.

Building Your Own Bin

Probably the best homemade composting design is the multiple bin system where separate compartments facilitate continuous decomposition. Each bin is about four feet on a side and three to four feet tall.

Usually, the dividing walls between bins are shared. Always, each bin opens completely at the front. I think the best design has removable slatted separators between a series of four (not three) wooden bins in three declining sizes: two large, one medium-large and one smaller. Alternatively, bins may be constructed of unmortared concrete blocks with removable wooden fronts. Permanently constructed bins of mortared concrete block or wood may have moisture-retentive, rain-protective hinged lids.

There are two workable composting systems that fit these structures. Most composters obtain materials too gradually to make a large heap all at once. In this case my suggestion is the four-bin system, using one large bin as a storage area for dry vegetation. Begin composting in bin two by mixing the dry contents temporarily stored in bin one with kitchen garbage, grass clippings and etc. Once bin two is filled and heating, remove its front slats and the side slats separating it from bin three and turn the pile into bin three, gradually reinserting side slats as bin three is filled. Bin three, being about two-thirds the size of bin two, will be filled to the brim. A new pile can be forming in bin two while bin three is cooking.

When bin three has settled significantly, repeat the process, turning bin three into bin four, etc. By the time the material has reheated in bin four and cooled you will have finished or close-to-finished compost At any point during this turning that resistant, unrotted material is discovered, instead of passing it on, it may be thrown back to an earlier bin to go through yet another decomposition stage. Perhaps the cleverest design of this type takes advantage of any significant slope or hill available to a lazy gardener and places a series of separate bins one above the next, eliminating any need for removable side-slats while making tossing compost down to the next container relatively easy.

A simply constructed alternative avoids making removable slats between bins or of lifting the material over the walls to toss it from bin to bin. Here, each bin is treated as a separate and discrete compost process. When it is time to turn the heap, the front is removed and the heap is turned right back into its original container. To accomplish this it may be necessary to first shovel about half of the material out of the bin onto a work area, then turn what is remaining in the bin and then cover it with what was shoveled out. Gradually the material in the bin shrinks and decomposes. When finished, the compost will fill only a small fraction of the bin's volume.

My clever students at the Urban Farm Class, University of Oregon have made a very inexpensive compost bin structure of this type using recycled industrial wood pallets. They are held erect by nailing them to pressure-treated fence posts sunk into the earth. The removable doors are also pallets, hooked on with bailing wire. The flimsy pallets rot in a couple of years but obtaining more free pallets is easy. If I were building a more finished three or four bin series, I would use rot-resistant wood like cedar and/or thoroughly paint the wood with a non-phytotoxic wood preservative like Cuprinol (copper napthanate). Cuprinol is not as permanent as other types of wood preservatives and may have to be reapplied every two or three years.

Bins reduce moisture loss and wood bins have the additional advantage of being fairly good thermal insulators: one inch of wood is as much insulation as one foot of solid concrete. Composting containers also have a potential disadvantage-reducing air flow, slowing decomposition, and possibly making the process go anaerobic. Should this happen air flow can be improved by supporting the heap on a slatted floor made of up-ended Cuprinol-treated 2 x 4's about three inches apart tacked into the back wall. Air ducts, inexpensively made from perforated plastic septic system leach line, are laid between the slats to greatly enhance air flow. I wouldn't initially build a bin array with ducted floors; these can be added as an afterthought if necessary.

Much simpler bins can be constructed out of 2" x 4" mesh x 36" or 48" high strong, welded wire fencing commonly called "turkey wire," or "hog wire." The fencing is formed into cylinders four to five feet in diameter. I think a serious gardener might need one five-foot circle and two, four-foot diameter ones. Turkey wire is stiff enough to support itself when formed into a circle by hooking the fencing upon itself. This home-rolled wire bin system is the least expensive of all.

As compostable materials are available, the wire circle is gradually filled. Once the bin has been loaded and has settled somewhat, the wire may be unhooked and peeled away; the material will hold itself in a cylindrical shape without further support. After a month or two the heap will have settled significantly and will be ready to be turned into a smaller wire cylinder. Again, the material is allowed to settle and then, if desired, the wire may be removed to be used again to form another neatly-shaped heap.

Wire-enclosed heaps encourage air circulation, but can also encourage drying out. Their proper location is in full shade. In hot, dry climates, moisture retention can be improved by wrapping a length of plastic sheeting around the outside of the circle and if necessary, by draping another plastic sheet over the top. However, doing this limits air flow and prevents removal of the wire support You may have to experiment with how much moisture-retention the heap can stand without going anaerobic. To calculate the length of wire (circumference) necessary to enclose any desired diameter, use the formula Circumference = Diameter x 3.14. For example, to make a five-foot circle: 5 x 3.14 = approximately 16 feet of wire.

With the exception of the "tumbler," commercially made compost bins are derived from one of these two systems. Usually the factory-made wire bins are formed into rectangles instead of circles and may be made of PVC coated steel instead of galvanized wire. I see no advantage in buying a wire bin over making one, other than supporting unnecessary stages of manufacture and distribution by spending more money. Turkey wire fencing is relatively inexpensive and easy enough to find at farm supply and fencing stores. The last time I purchased any it was sold by the lineal foot much as hardware cloth is dispensed at hardware and building supply stores.

Manufactured solid-sided bins are usually constructed of sheet steel or recycled plastic. In cool climates there is an advantage to tightly constructed plastic walls that retain heat and facilitate decomposition of smaller thermal masses. Precise construction also prevents access by larger vermin and pets. Mice, on the other hand, are capable of squeezing through amazingly small openings. Promotional materials make composting in pre-manufactured bins seem easy, self righteously ecological, and effortless. However, there are drawbacks.

It is not possible to readily turn the materials once they've been placed into most composters of this type unless the entire front is removable. Instead, new materials are continuously placed on top while an opening at the bottom permits the gardener to scrape out finished compost in small quantities. Because no turning is involved, this method is called "passive" composting. But to work well, the ingredients must not be too coarse and must be well mixed before loading.

Continuous bin composters generally work fast enough when processing *mixtures* of readily decomposable materials like kitchen garbage, weeds, grass clippings and some leaves. But if the load contains too much fine grass or other gooey stuff and goes anaerobic, a special compost aerator must be used to loosen it up.

Manufactured passive composters are not very large. Compactness may be an advantage to people with very small yards or who may want to compost on their terrace or porch. But if the C/N of the materials is not favorable, decomposition can take a long, long time and several bins may have to be used in tandem. Unless they are first ground or chopped very finely, larger more resistant materials like corn, Brussels sprouts, sunflower stalks, cabbage stumps, shrub prunings, etc. will "constipate" a top-loading, bottom-discharging composter.

The compost tumbler is a clever method that accelerates decomposition by improving aeration and facilitating frequent turning. A rotating drum holding from eight to eighteen bushels (the larger sizes look like a squat, fat, oversized oil drum) is suspended above the ground, top-loaded with organic matter, and then tumbled every few days for a few weeks until the materials have decomposed. Then the door is opened and finished compost falls out the bottom.

Tumblers have real advantages. Frequent turning greatly increases air supply and accelerates the process. Most tumblers retard moisture loss too because they are made of solid material, either heavy plastic or steel with small air vents. Being suspended above ground makes them immune to vermin and frequent turning makes it impossible for flies to breed.

Tumblers have disadvantages that may not become apparent until a person has used one for awhile. First, although greatly accelerated, composting in them is not instantaneous. Passive bins are continuous processors while (with the exception of one unique design) tumblers are "batch" processors, meaning that they are first loaded and then the entire load is decomposed to finished compost. What does a person do with newly acquired kitchen garbage and other waste during the two to six weeks that they are tumbling a batch? One handy solution is to buy two tumblers and be filling one while the other is working, but tumblers aren't cheap! The more substantial ones cost $250 to $400 plus freight.

There are other less obvious tumbler disadvantages that may negate any work avoided, time saved, or sweaty turning with a manure fork eliminated. Being top-loaded means lifting compost materials and dropping them into a small opening that may be shoulder height or more. These materials may include a sloppy bucket of kitchen garbage. Then, a tumbler *must* be tumbled for a few minutes every two or three days. Cranking the lever or grunting with the barrel may seem like fun at first but it can get old fast. Decomposition in an untumbled tumbler slows down to a crawl.

Both the passive compost bin and the highly active compost tumbler work much better when loaded with small-sized particles. The purchase of either one tends to impel the gardener to also buy something to cut and/or grind compost materials.

The U.C. Method—Grinder/Shredders

During the 1950s, mainstream interest in municipal composting developed in America for the first time. Various industrial processes already existed in Europe; most of these were patented variations on large and expensive composting tumblers. Researchers at the University of California set out to see if simpler methods could be developed to handle urban organic wastes without investing in so much heavy machinery.

Their best system, named the U. C. Fast Compost Method, rapidly made compost in about two weeks.

No claim was ever made that U. C. method produces the highest quality compost. The idea was to process and decompose organic matter as inoffensively and rapidly as possible. No attempt is made to maximize the product's C/N as is done in slower methods developed by Howard at Indore. Most municipal composting done in this country today follows the basic process worked out by the University of California.

Speed of decomposition comes about from very high internal heat and extreme aerobic conditions. To achieve the highest possible temperature, all of the organic material to be composted is first passed through a grinder and then stacked in a long, high windrow. Generally the height is about five to six feet, any higher causes too much compaction. Because the material is stacked with sides as vertical as possible, the width takes care of itself.

Frequent turning with machinery keeps the heap working rapidly. During the initial experiments the turning was done with a tractor and front end loader. These days giant "U" shaped machines may roll down windrows at municipal composting plots, automatically turning, reshaping the windrow and if necessary, simultaneously spraying water.

Some municipal waste consists of moist kitchen garbage and grass clippings. Most of the rest is dry paper. If this mixture results in a moisture content that is too high the pile gets soggy, sags promptly, and easily goes anaerobic. Turning not only restores aerobic conditions, but also tends to drop the moisture content. If the initial moisture content is between 60 and 70 percent, the windrow is turned every two days. Five such turns, starting two days after the windrow is first formed, finishes the processing. If the moisture content is between 10 and 60 percent, the windrow is first turned after three days and thence at three day intervals, taking about four turns to finish the process. If the moisture content is below 40 percent or drops below 40 percent during processing, moisture is added.

No nuisances can develop if turning is done correctly. Simply flipping the heap over or adding new material on top will not do it. The material must be blended so that the outsides are shifted to the core and the core becomes the skin. This way, any fly larvae, pathogens, or insect eggs that might not be killed by the cooler temperatures on the outside are rotated into the lethal high heat of the core every few days.

The speed of the U.C. method also appeals to the backyard gardener. At home, frequent turning can be accomplished either in naked heaps, or by switching from one bin to the next and back, or with a compost tumbler. But a chipper/shredder is also essential. Grinding everything that goes into the heap has other advantages than higher heat and accelerated processing. Materials may be initially mixed as they are ground and small particles are much easier to turn over than long twigs, tough straw, and other fibrous materials that tie the heap together and make it difficult to separate and handle with hand tools.

Backyard shredders have other uses, especially for gardeners with no land to waste. Composting tough materials like grape prunings, berry canes, and hedge trimmings can take a long time. Slow heaps containing resistant materials occupy precious space. With a shredder you can fast-compost small limbs, tree prunings, and other woody materials like corn and sunflower stalks. Whole autumn leaves tend to compact into airless layers and decompose slowly, but dry leaves are among the easiest of all materials to grind. Once smashed into flakes, leaves become a fluffy material that resists compaction.

Electric driven garden chipper/shredders are easier on the neighbors' ears than more powerful gasoline-powered machines, although not so quiet that I'd run one without ear protection. Electrics are light enough for a strong person to pick up and carry out to the composting area and keep secured in a storeroom. One more plus, there never is any problem starting an electric motor. But no way to conveniently repair one either.

There are two basic shredding systems. One is the hammermill—a grinding chamber containing a rotating spindle with steel tines or hammers attached that repeatedly beats and tears materials into smaller and smaller pieces until they fall out through a bottom screen. Hammermills will flail almost anything to pieces without becoming dulled. Soft, green materials are beaten to shreds; hard, dry, brittle stuff is rapidly fractured into tiny chips. Changing the size of the discharge screen adjusts the size of the final product. By using very coarse screens, even soft, wet, stringy materials can be slowly fed through the grinding chamber without hopelessly tangling up in the hammers.

Like a coarse power planer in a wood shop, the other type of machine uses sharpened blades that slice thin chips from whatever is pushed into its maw. The chipper is designed to grind woody materials like small tree limbs, prunings, and berry canes. Proper functioning depends on having sharp blades. But edges easily become dulled and require maintenance. Care must be taken to avoid passing soil and small stones through a chipper. Soft, dry, brittle materials like leaves will be broken up but aren't processed as rapidly as in a hammermill. Chippers won't handle soft wet stuff.

When driven by low horsepower electric motors, both chippers and hammermills are light duty machines. They may be a little shaky, standing on spindly legs or small platforms, so materials must be fed in gently. Most electric models cost between $300 and $400.

People with more than a postage-stamp yard who like dealing with machinery may want a gasoline-powered shredder/chipper. These are much more substantial machines that combine both a big hammermill shredder with a side-feeding chipper for limbs and branches. Flailing within a hammermill or chipping limbs of two or more inches in diameter focuses a great deal of force; between the engine noise and the deafening din as dry materials bang around the grinding chamber, ear protection is essential. So are safety goggles and heavy gloves. Even though the fan belt driving the spindle is shielded, I would not operate one without wearing tight-fitting clothes. When grinding dry materials, great clouds of dust may be given off. Some of these particles, like the dust from alfalfa or from dried-out spoiled (moldy) hay, can severely irritate lungs, eyes, throat and nasal passages. A face mask, or better, an army surplus gas mask with built-in goggles, may be in order. And you'll probably want to take a shower when finished.

Fitted with the right-size screen selected from the assortment supplied at purchase, something learned after a bit of experience, powerful hammermills are capable of pulverizing fairly large amounts of dry material in short order. But wet stuff is much slower to pass through and may take a much coarser screen to get out at all. Changing materials may mean changing screens and that takes a few minutes. Dry leaves seem to flow through as fast as they can be fed in. The sidefeed auxiliary chippers incorporated into hammermills will make short work of smaller green tree limbs; but dry, hardened wood takes a lot longer. Feeding large hard branches too fast can tear up chipper blades and even break the ball-bearing housings holding the spindle. Here I speak from experience.

Though advertisements for these machines make them seem effortless and fast, shredders actually take considerable time, energy, skilled attention, constant concentration, and experience. When grinding one must attentively match the inflow to the rate of outflow because if the hopper is overfilled the tines become snarled and cease to work. For example, tangling easily can occur while rapidly feeding in thin brittle flakes of dry spoiled hay and then failing to slow down while a soft, wet flake is gradually reduced. To clear a snarled rotor without risking continued attachment of one's own arm, the motor must be killed before reaching into the hopper and untangling the tines. To clear badly clogged machines it may also be necessary to first remove and then replace the discharge screen, something that takes a few minutes.

There are significant differences in the quality of materials and workmanship that go into making these machines. They all look good when freshly painted; it is not always possible to know what you have bought until a season or two of heavy use has passed. One tried-and-true aid to choosing quality is to ask equipment rental businesses what brand their customers are not able to destroy. Another guide is to observe the brand of gasoline engine attached.

In my gardening career I've owned quite a few gas-powered rotary tillers and lawnmowers and one eight-horsepower shredder. In my experience there are two grades of small gasoline engines—"consumer" and the genuine "industrial." Like all consumer merchandise, consumer-grade engines are intended to be consumed. They have a design life of a few hundred hours and then are worn out. Most parts are made of soft, easily-machined aluminum, reinforced with small amounts of steel in vital places.

There are two genuinely superior American companies—Kohler and Wisconsin-that make very durable, long-lasting gas engines commonly found on small industrial equipment. With proper maintenance their machines are designed to endure thousands of hours of continuous use. I believe small gas engines made by Yamaha, Kawasaki, and especially Honda, are of equal or greater quality to anything made in America. I suggest you could do worse than to judge how long the maker expects their shredder/chipper to last by the motor it selects.

Gasoline-powered shredder/chippers cost from $700 to $1,300. Back in the early 1970s I wore one pretty well out in only one year of making fast compost for a half-acre Biodynamic French intensive market garden. When I amortized the cost of the machine into the value of both the compost and the vegetables I grew with the compost, and considered the amount of time I spent running the grinder against the extra energy it takes to turn ordinary slow compost heaps I decided I would be better off allowing my heaps to take more time to mature.

Sheet Composting

Decomposition happens rapidly in a hot compost heap with the main agents of decay being heat-loving microorganisms. Decomposition happens slowly at the soil's surface with the main agents of decay being soil animals. However, if the leaves and forest duff on the floor of a forest or a thick matted sod are tilled into the topsoil, decomposition is greatly accelerated.

For two centuries, frontier American agriculture depended on just such a method. Early pioneers would move into an untouched region, clear the forest, and plow in millennia of accumulated nutrients held as biomass on the forest floor. For a few years, perhaps a decade, or even twenty years if the soil carried a higher level of mineralization than the average, crops from forest soils grew magnificently. Then, unless other methods were introduced to rebuild fertility, yields, crop, animal, and human health all declined. When the less-leached grassy prairies of what we now call the Midwest were reached, even greater bounties were mined out for more years because rich black-soil grasslands contain more mineral nutrients and sod accumulates far more humus than do forests.

Sheet composting mimics this system while saving a great deal of effort. Instead of first heaping organic matter up, turning it several times, carting humus back to the garden, spreading it, and tilling it in, sheet composting conducts the decomposition process with far less effort right in the soil needing enrichment.

Sheet composting is the easiest method of all. However, the method has certain liabilities. Unless the material being spread is pure manure without significant amounts of bedding, or only fresh spring grass clippings, or alfalfa hay, the carbon-nitrogen ratio will almost certainly be well above that of stable humus. As explained earlier, during the initial stages of decay the soil will be thoroughly depleted of nutrients. Only after the surplus carbon has been consumed will the soil ecology and nutrient profile normalize. The time this will take depends on the nature of the materials being composted and on soil conditions.

If the soil is moist, airy, and warm and if it already contained high levels of nutrients, and if the organic materials are not ligneous and tough and have a reasonable C/N, then sheet composting will proceed rapidly. If the soil is cold, dry, clayey (relatively airless) or infertile and/or the organic matter consists of things like grain straw, paper, or the very worst, barkless sawdust, then decomposition will be slowed. Obviously, it is not possible to state with any precision how fast sheet composting would proceed for you.

Autumn leaves usually sheet compost very successfully. These are gathered, spread over all of the garden (except for those areas intended for early spring sowing), and tilled in as shallowly as possible before winter. Even in the North where soil freezes solid for months, some decomposition will occur in autumn and then in spring, as the soil warms, composting instantly resumes and is finished by the time frost danger is over. Sheet composting higher C/N materials in spring is also workable where the land is not scheduled for planting early. If the organic matter has a low C/N, like manure, a tender green manure crop not yet forming seed, alfalfa hay or grass clippings, quite a large volume of material can be decomposed by warm soil in a matter of weeks.

However, rotting large quantities of very resistant material like sawdust can take many months, even in hot, moist soil. Most gardeners cannot afford to give their valuable land over to being a compost factory for months. One way to speed the sheet composting of something with a high C/N is to amend it with a strong nitrogen source like chicken manure or seed meal. If sawdust is the only organic matter you can find, I recommend an exception to avoiding chemical fertilizer. By adding about 80 pounds of urea to each cubic yard of sawdust, its overall C/N is reduced from 500:1 to about 20:1. Urea is perhaps the most benign of all chemical nitrogen sources. It does not acidify the soil, is not toxic to worms or other soil animals or microorganisms, and is actually a synthetic form of the naturally occurring chemical that contains most of the nitrogen in animal urine. In that sense, putting urea in soil is not that different than putting synthetic vitamin C in a human body.

Burying kitchen garbage is a traditional form of sheet composting practiced by row-cropping gardeners usually in mild climates where the soil does not freeze in winter. Some people use a post hole digger to make a neat six- to eight-inch diameter hole about eighteen inches deep between well-spaced growing rows of plants. When the hole has been filled to within two or three inches of the surface, it is topped off with soil. Rarely will animals molest buried garbage, it is safe from flies and yet enough air exists in the soil for it to rapidly decompose. The local soil ecology and nutrient balance is temporarily disrupted, but the upset only happens in this one little spot far enough away from growing plants to have no harmful effect.

Another garbage disposal variation has been called "trench composting." Instead of a post hole, a long trench about the width of a combination shovel and a foot deep is gradually dug between row crops spaced about four feet (or more) apart. As bucket after bucket of garbage, manure, and other organic matter are emptied into the trench, it is covered with soil dug from a little further along. Next year, the rows are shifted two feet over so that crops are sown above the composted garbage.

Mulch Gardening

Ruth Stout discovered—or at least popularized this new-to-her method. Mulching may owe some of its popularity to Ruth's possession of writing talent similar to her brother Rex's, who was a well-known mid-century mystery writer. Ruth's humorous book, *Gardening Without Work* is a fun-to-read classic that I highly recommend if for no other reason than it shows how an intelligent person can make remarkable discoveries simply by observing the obvious. However, like many other garden writers, Ruth Stout made the mistake of assuming that what worked in her own backyard would be universally applicable. Mulch gardening does not succeed everywhere.

This easy method mimics decomposition on the forest floor. Instead of making compost heaps or sheet composting, the garden is kept thickly covered with a permanent layer of decomposing vegetation. Year-round mulch produces a number of synergistic advantages. Decay on the soil's surface is slow but steady and maintains fertility. As on the forest floor, soil animals and worm populations are high. Their activities continuously loosen the earth, steadily transport humus and nutrients deeper into the soil, and eliminate all need for tillage. Protected from the sun, the surface layers of soil do not dry out so shallow-feeding species like lettuce and moisture-lovers like radishes make much better growth. During high summer, mulched ground does not become unhealthfully heated up either.

The advantages go on. The very top layer of soil directly under the mulch has a high organic matter content, retaining moisture, eliminating crusting, and consequently, enhancing the germination of seeds. Mulchers usually sow in well-separated rows. The gardener merely rakes back the mulch and exposes a few inches of bare soil, scratches a furrow, and covers the seed with humusy topsoil. As the seedlings grow taller and are thinned out, the mulch is gradually pushed back around them.

Weeds? No problem! Except where germinating seeds, the mulch layer is thick enough to prevent weed seeds from sprouting. Should a weed begin showing through the mulch, this is taken as an indication that spot has become too thinly covered and a flake of spoiled hay or other vegetation is tossed on the unwanted plant, smothering it.

Oh, how easy it seems! Pick a garden site. If you have a year to wait before starting your garden do not even bother to till first. Cover it a foot deep with combinations of spoiled hay, leaves, grass clippings, and straw. Woody wastes are not suitable because they won't rot fast enough to feed the soil. Kitchen garbage and manures can also be tossed on the earth and, for a sense of tidiness, covered with hay. The mulch smothers the grass or weeds growing there and the site begins to soften. Next year it will be ready to grow vegetables.

If the plot is very infertile to begin with there won't be enough biological activity or nutrients in the soil to rapidly decompose the mulch. In that case, to accelerate the process, before first putting down mulch till in an initial manure layer or a heavy sprinkling of seed meal. Forever after, mulching materials alone will be sufficient. Never again till. Never again weed. Never again fertilize. No compost piles to make, turn, and haul. Just keep your eye open for spoiled hay and buy a few inexpensive tons of it each year.

Stout, who discovered mulch gardening in Connecticut where irregular summer rains were usually sufficient to water a widely-spaced garden, also mistakenly thought that mulched gardens lost less soil moisture because the earth was protected from the drying sun and thus did not need irrigation through occasional drought. I suspect that drought resistance under mulch has more to do with a plant's ability to feed vigorously, obtain nutrition, and continue growing because the surface inches where most of soil nutrients and biological activities are located, stayed moist. I also suspect that actual, measurable moisture loss from mulched soil may be greater than from bare earth. But that's another book I wrote, called *Gardening Without Irrigation*.

Yes, gardening under permanent year-round mulch seems easy, but it does have a few glitches. Ruth Stout did not discover them because she lived in Connecticut where the soil freezes solid every winter and stays frozen for long enough to set back population levels of certain soil animals. In the North, earwigs and sow bugs (pill bugs) are frequently found in mulched gardens but they do not become a serious pest. Slugs are infrequent and snails don't exist. All thanks to winter.

Try permanent mulch in the deep South, or California where I was first disappointed with mulching, or the Maritime northwest where I now live, and a catastrophe develops. During the first year these soil animals are present but cause no problem. But after the first mild winter with no population setback, they become a plague. Slugs (and in California, snails) will be found everywhere, devastating seedlings. Earwigs and sow bugs, that previously only were seen eating only decaying mulch, begin to attack plants. It soon becomes impossible to get a stand of seedlings established. The situation can be rapidly cured by raking up all the mulch, carting it away from the garden, and composting it. I know this to be the truth because I've had to do just that both in California where as a novice gardener I had my first mulch catastrophes, and then when I moved to Oregon, I gave mulching another trial with similar sad results.

Chapter 6

Vermicomposting

It was 1952 and Mr. Campbell had a worm bin. This shallow box—about two feet wide by four feet long—resided under a worktable in the tiny storeroom/greenhouse adjacent to our grade school science class. It was full of what looked like black, crumbly soil and zillions of small, red wiggly worms, not at all like the huge nightcrawlers I used to snatch from the lawn after dark to take fishing the next morning. Mr. Campbell's worms were fed used coffee grounds; the worms in turn were fed to salamanders, to Mr. Campbell's favorite fish, a fourteen-inch long smallmouth bass named Carl, to various snakes, and to turtles living in aquariums around the classroom. From time to time the "soil" in the box was fed to his lush potted plants.

Mr. Campbell was vermicomposting. This being before the age of ecology and recycling, he probably just thought of it as raising live food to sustain his educational menagerie. Though I never had reason to raise worms before, preparing to write this book perked my interest in every possible method of composting. Not comfortable writing about something I had not done, I built a small worm box, obtained a pound or so of brandling worms, made bedding, added worms, and began feeding the contents of my kitchen compost bucket to the box.

To my secret surprise, vermicomposting works just as Mary Appel-hof's book *Worms Eat My Garbage* said it would. Worm composting is amazingly easy, although I admit there was a short learning curve and a few brief spells of sour odors that went away as soon as I stopped overfeeding the worms. I also discovered that my slapdash homemade box had to have a drip catching pan beneath it. A friend of mine, who has run her own in-the-house worm box for years, tells me that diluting these occasional, insignificant and almost odorless dark-colored liquid emissions with several parts water makes them into excellent fertilizer for house plants or garden.

It quickly became clear to me that composting with worms conveniently solves several recycling glitches. How does a northern home-owner process kitchen garbage in the winter when the ground and compost pile are frozen and there is no other vegetation to mix in? And can an apartment dweller without any other kind of organic waste except garbage and perhaps newspaper recycle these at home? The solution to both situations is vermicomposting.

Worm castings, the end product of vermicomposting, are truly the finest compost you could make or buy. Compared to the volume of kitchen waste that will go into a worm box, the amount of castings you end up with will be small, though potent. Apartment dwellers could use worm castings to raise magnificent house plants or scatter surplus casts under the ornamentals or atop the lawn around their buildings or in the local park.

In this chapter, I encourage you to at least try worm composting. I also answer the questions that people ask the most about using worms to recycle kitchen garbage. As the ever-enthusiastic Mary Applehof said:

I hope it convinces you that you, too, can vermicompost, and that this simple process with the funny name is a lot easier to do than you thought. After all, if worms eat my garbage, they will eat yours, too.

Locating the Worms

The species of worm used for vermicomposting has a number of common names: red worms, red wigglers, manure worms, or brandling worms. Red worms are healthy and active as long as they are kept above freezing and below 85°. Even if the air temperature gets above 85°, their moist bedding will be cooled by evaporation as long as air circulation is adequate. They are most active and will consume the most waste between 55–77°. Red worms need to live in a moist environment but must breath air through their skin. Keeping their bedding damp is rarely the problem; preventing it from becoming waterlogged and airless can be a difficulty.

In the South or along the Pacific coast where things never freeze solid, worms may be kept outside in a shallow shaded pit (as long as the spot does not become flooded) or in a box in the garage or patio. In the North, worms are kept in a container that may be located anywhere with good ventilation and temperatures that stay above freezing but do not get too hot. Good spots for a worm box are under the kitchen sink, in the utility room, or in the basement. The kitchen, being the source of the worm's food, is the most convenient, except for the danger of temporary odors.

If you have one, a basement may be the best location because it is out of the way. While you are learning to manage your worms there may be occasional short-term odor problems or fruit flies; these won't be nearly as objectionable if the box is below the house. Then too, a vermicomposter can only exist in a complex ecology of soil animals. A few of these may exit the box and be harmlessly found about the kitchen. Ultra-fastidious housekeepers may find this objectionable. Basements also tend to maintain a cooler temperature in summer. However, it is less convenient to take the compost bucket down to the basement every few days.

Containers

Red worms need to breathe oxygen, but in deep containers bedding can pack down and become airless, temporarily preventing the worms from eating the bottom material. This might not be so serious because you will stir up the box from time to time when adding new food. But anaerobic decomposition smells bad. If aerobic conditions are maintained, the odor from a worm box is very slight and not particularly objectionable. I notice the box's odor only when I am adding new garbage and get my nose up close while stirring the material. A shallow box will be better aerated because it exposes much more surface area. Worm bins should be from eight to twelve inches deep.

I constructed my own box out of some old plywood. A top is not needed because the worms will not crawl out. In fact, when worm composting is done outdoors in shallow pits, few red worms exit the bottom by entering the soil because there is little there for them to eat. Because air flow is vital, numerous holes between 1/4 and 1/2 inch in diameter should be made in the bottom and the box must then have small legs or cleats about 1/2 to 3/4 of an inch thick to hold it up enough to let air flow beneath. Having a drip-catcher—a large cookie tray works well—is essential. Worms can also be kept in plastic containers (like dish pans) with holes punched in the bottom. As this book is being written, one mail-order garden supply company even sells a tidy-looking 19" by 24" by about 12" deep green plastic vermicomposting bin with drip pan, lid, and an initial supply of worms and bedding. If worm composting becomes more popular, others will follow suit.

Unless you are very strong do not construct a box larger than 2 x 4 feet because they will need to be lifted from time to time. Wooden boxes should last three or four years. If built of plywood, use an exterior grade to prevent delamination. It is not advisable to make containers from rot-resistant redwood or cedar because the natural oils that prevent rotting also may be toxic to worms. Sealed with polyurethane, epoxy, or other non-toxic waterproofing material, worm boxes should last quite a bit longer.

How big a box or how many boxes do you need? Each cubic foot of worm box can process about one pound of kitchen garbage each week. Naturally, some weeks more garbage will go into the box than others. The worms will adjust to such changes. You can estimate box size by a weekly average amount of garbage over a three month time span. My own home-garden-supplied kitchen feeds two "vegetableatarian" adults. Being year-round gardeners, our kitchen discards a lot of trimmings that would never leave a supermarket and we throw out as "old," salad greens that are still fresher than most people buy in the store. I'd say our 2½ gallon compost bucket is dumped twice a week in winter and three times in summer. From May through September while the garden is "on," a single, 2 foot x 4 foot by 12 inch tall (8 cubic foot) box is not enough for us .

Bedding

Bedding is a high C/N material that holds moisture, provides an aerobic medium worms can exist in, and allows you to bury the garbage in the box. The best beddings are also light and airy, helping to maintain aerobic conditions. Bedding must not be toxic to worms because they'll eventually eat it. Bedding starts out dry and must be first soaked in water and then squeezed out until it is merely very damp. Several ordinary materials make fine bedding. You may use a single material bedding or may come to prefer mixtures.

If you have a power shredder, you can grind corrugated cardboard boxes. Handling ground up cardboard indoors may be a little dusty until you moisten it. Shredded cardboard is sold in bulk as insulation but this material has been treated with a fire retardant that is toxic. Gasoline powered shredders can also grind up cereal straw or spoiled grass hay (if it is dry and brittle). Alfalfa hay will decompose too rapidly.

Similarly, shredded newsprint makes fine bedding. The ink is not toxic, being made from carbon black and oil. By tearing with the grain, entire newspaper sections can rapidly be ripped into inch-wide shreds by hand. Other shredded paper may be available from banks, offices, or universities that may dispose of documents.

Ground-up leaves make terrific bedding. Here a power shredder is not necessary. An ordinary lawnmower is capable of chopping and bagging large volumes of dry leaves in short order. These may be prepared once a year and stored dry in plastic garbage bags until needed. A few 30gallon bags will handle your vermicomposting for an entire year. However, dry leaves may be a little slower than other materials to rehydrate.

Peat moss is widely used as bedding by commercial worm growers. It is very acid and contains other substances harmful to worms that are first removed by soaking the moss for a few hours and then hand-squeezing the soggy moss until it is damp. Then a little lime is added to adjust the pH.

Soil

Red worms are heat-tolerant litter dwellers that find little to eat in soil. Mixing large quantities of soil into worm bedding makes a very heavy box. However, the digestive system of worms grinds food using soil particles as the abrasive grit in the same way birds "chew" in their crop. A big handful of added soil will improve a worm box. A couple of tablespoonfuls of powdered agricultural lime does the same thing while adding additional calcium to nourish the worms.

Red worms

The scientific name of the species used in vermicomposting is *Eisenia foetida*. They may be purchased by mail from breeders, from bait stores, and these days, even from mail-order garden supply companies. Red worms may also be collected from compost and manure piles after they have heated and are cooling.

Nightcrawlers and common garden worms play a very important part in the creation and maintenance of soil fertility. But these species are soil dwellers that require cool conditions. They cannot survive in a shallow worm box at room temperatures.

Red worms are capable of very rapid reproduction at room temperatures in a worm box. They lay eggs encased in a lemon-shaped cocoon about the size of a grain of rice from which baby worms will hatch. The cocoons start out pearly white but as the baby worms develop over a three week period, the eggs change color to yellow, then light brown, and finally are reddish when the babies are ready to hatch. Normally, two or three young worms emerge from a cocoon.

Hatchlings are whitish and semi-transparent and about one-half inch long. It would take about 150,000 hatchlings to weigh one pound. A red worm hatchling will grow at an explosive rate and reach sexual maturity in four to six weeks. Once it begins breeding a red worm makes two to three cocoons a week for six months to a year; or, one breeding worm can make about 100 babies in six months. And the babies are breeding about three months after the first eggs are laid.

Though this reproductive rate is not the equal of yeast (capable of doubling every twenty minutes), still a several-hundred-fold increase every six months is amazingly fast. When vermicomposting, the worm population increase is limited by available food and space and by the worms' own waste products or casts. Worm casts are slightly toxic to worms. When a new box starts out with fresh bedding it contains no casts. As time goes on, the bedding is gradually broken down by cellulose-eating microorganisms whose decay products are consumed by the worms and the box gradually fills with casts.

As the proportion of casts increases, reproduction slows, and mature worms begin to die. However, you will almost never see a dead worm in a worm box because their high-protein bodies are rapidly decomposed. You will quickly recognize worm casts. Once the bedding has been consumed and the box contains only worms, worm casts, and fresh garbage it is necessary to empty the casts, replace the bedding, and start the cycle over. How to do this will be explained in a moment. But first, how many worms will you need to begin vermicomposting?

You could start with a few dozen red worms, patiently begin by feeding them tiny quantities of garbage and in six months to a year have a box full. However, you'll almost certainly want to begin with a system that can consume all or most of your kitchen garbage right away. So for starters you'll need to obtain two pounds of worms for each pound of garbage you'll put into the box each day. Suppose in an average week your kitchen compost bucket takes in seven pounds of waste or about one gallon. That averages one pound per day. You'll need about two pounds of worms.

You'll also need a box that holds six or seven cubic feet, or about 2 x 3 feet by 12 inches deep. Each pound of worms needs three or four cubic feet of bedding. A better way to estimate box size is to figure that one cubic foot of worm bin can digest about one pound of kitchen waste a week without going anaerobic and smelling bad.

Red worms are small and consequently worm growers sell them by the pound. There are about 1,000 mature breeders to the pound of young red worms. Bait dealers prefer to sell only the largest sizes or their customers complain. "Red wigglers" from a bait store may only count 600 to the pound. Worm raisers will sell "pit run" that costs much less. This is a mix of worms of all sizes and ages. Often the largest sizes will have already been separated out for sale as fish bait. That's perfectly okay. Since hatchlings run 150,000 to the pound and mature worms count about 600–700, the population of a pound of pit run can vary greatly. A reasonable pit run estimate is 2,000 to the pound.

Actually it doesn't matter what the number is, it is their weight that determines how much they'll eat. Red worms eat slightly more than their weight in food every day. If that is so, why did I recommend first starting vermicomposting with two pounds of worms for every pound of garbage? Because the worms you'll buy will not be used to living in the kind of bedding you'll give them nor adjusted to the mix of garbage you'll feed them. Initially there may be some losses. After a few weeks the surviving worms will have adjusted.

Most people have little tolerance for outright failure. But if they have a record of successes behind them, minor glitches won't stop them. So it is vital to start with enough worms. The *only time vermicomposting becomes odoriferous is when the worms are fed too much.* If they quickly eat all the food that they are given the system runs remarkably smoothly and makes no offense. Please keep that in mind since there may well be some short-lived problems until you learn to gauge their intake.

Setting Up a Worm Box

Red worms need a damp but not soggy environment with a moisture content more or less 75 percent by weight. But bedding material starts out very dry. So weigh the bedding and then add three times that weight of water. The rule to remember here is "a pint's a pound the world 'round," or one gallon of water weighs about eight pounds. As a gauge, it takes 1 to 1½ pounds of dry bedding for each cubic foot of box.

Preparing bedding material can be a messy job The best container is probably an empty garbage can, though in a pinch it can be done in a kitchen sink or a couple of five gallon plastic buckets. Cautiously put half the (probably dusty) bedding in the mixing container. Add about one-half the needed water and mix thoroughly. Then add two handfuls of soil, the rest of the bedding, and the balance of the water. Continue mixing until all the water has been absorbed. Then spread the material evenly through your empty worm box. If you've measured correctly no water should leak out the bottom vent holes and the bedding should not drip when a handful is squeezed moderately hard.

Then add the worms. Spread your red worms over the surface of the bedding. They'll burrow under the surface to avoid the light and in a few minutes will be gone. Then add garbage. When you do this the first time, I suggest that you spread the garbage over the entire surface and mix it in using a three-tined hand cultivator. This is the best tool to work the box with because the rounded points won't cut worms.

Then cover the box. Mary Applehof suggests using a black plastic sheet slightly smaller than the inside dimensions of the container. Black material keeps out light and allows the worms to be active right on the surface. You may find that a plastic covering retains too much moisture and overly restricts air flow. When I covered my worm box with plastic it dripped too much. But then, most of what I feed the worms is fresh vegetable material that runs 80–90 percent water. Other households may feed dryer material like stale bread and leftovers. I've found that on our diet it is better to keep the box in a dimly lit place and to use a single sheet of newspaper folded to the inside dimensions of the box as a loose cover that encourages aeration, somewhat reduces light on the surface, and lessens moisture loss yet does not completely stop it.

Feeding the Worms

Red worms will thrive on any kind of vegetable waste you create while preparing food. Here's a partial list to consider: potato peelings, citrus rinds, the outer leaves of lettuce and cabbage, spinach stems, cabbage and cauliflower cores, celery butts, plate scrapings, spoiled food like old baked beans, moldy cheese and other leftovers, tea bags, egg shells, juicer pulp. The worms' absolute favorite seems to be used coffee grounds though these can ferment and make a sour smell.

Drip coffee lovers can put the filters in too. This extra paper merely supplements the bedding. Large pieces of vegetable matter can take a long time to be digested. Before tossing cabbage or cauliflower cores or celery butts into the compost bucket, cut them up into finer chunks or thin slices. It is not necessary to grind the garbage. Everything will break down eventually.

Putting meat products into a worm box may be a mistake. The odors from decaying meat can be foul and it has been known to attract mice and rats. Small quantities cut up finely and well dispersed will digest neatly. Bones are slow to decompose in a worm box. If you spread the worm casts as compost it may not look attractive containing whitened, picked-clean bones. Chicken bones are soft and may disappear during vermicomposting. If you could grind bones before sending them to the worm bin, they would make valuable additions to your compost. Avoid putting non-biodegradable items like plastic, bottle caps, rubber bands, aluminum foil, and glass into the worm box.

Do not let your cat use the worm bin as a litter box.. The odor of cat urine would soon become intolerable while the urine is so high in nitrogen that it might kill some worms. Most seriously, cat manure can transmit the cysts of a protozoan disease organism called *Toxoplasma gondii*, although most cats do not carry the disease. These parasites may also be harbored in adult humans without them feeling any ill effects. However, transmitted from mother to developing fetus, *Toxoplasma gondii* can cause brain damage. You are going to handle the contents of your worm bin and won't want to take a chance on being infected with these parasites.

Most people use some sort of plastic jar, recycled half-gallon yogurt tub, empty waxed paper milk carton, or similar thing to hold kitchen garbage. Odors develop when anaerobic decomposition begins. If the holding tub is getting high, don't cover it, feed it to the worms.

It is neater to add garbage in spots rather than mixing it throughout the bin. When feeding garbage into the worm bin, lift the cover, pull back the bedding with a three-tine hand cultivator, and make a hole about the size of your garbage container. Dump the waste into that hole and cover it with an inch or so of bedding. The whole operation only takes a few minutes. A few days later the kitchen compost bucket will again be ready. Make and fill another hole adjacent to the first. Methodically go around the box this way. By the time you get back to the first spot the garbage will have become unrecognizable, the spot will seem to contain mostly worm casts and bedding, and will not give off strongly unpleasant odors when disturbed.

Seasonal Overloads

On festive occasions, holidays, and during canning season it is easy to overload the digestive capacity of a worm bin. The problem will correct itself without doing anything but you may not be willing to live with anaerobic odors for a week or two. One simple way to accelerate the "healing" of an anaerobic box is to fluff it up with your hand cultivator.

Vegetableatarian households greatly increase the amount of organic waste they generate during summer. So do people who can or freeze when the garden is "on." One vermicomposting solution to this seasonal overload is to start up a second, summertime-only outdoor worm bin in the garage or other shaded location.

Appelhof uses an old, leaky galvanized washtub for this purpose. The tub gets a few inches of fresh bedding and then is inoculated with a gallon of working vermicompost from the original bin. Extra garbage goes in all summer. Mary says:

I have used for a "worm bin annex" an old leaky galvanized washtub, kept outside near the garage. During canning season the grape pulp, corn cobs, corn husks, bean cuttings and other fall harvest residues went into the container. It got soggy when it rained and the worms got huge from all the food and moisture. We brought it inside at about the time of the first frost. The worms kept working the material until there was no food left. After six to eight months, the only identifiable remains were a few corn cobs, squash seeds, tomato skins and some undecomposed corn husks. The rest was an excellent batch of worm castings and a very few hardy, undernourished worms.

Vacations

Going away from home for a few weeks is not a problem. The worms will simply continue eating the garbage left in the bin. Eventually their food supply will decline enough that the population will drop. This will remedy itself as soon as you begin feeding the bin again. If a month or more is going to pass without adding food or if the house will be unheated during a winter "sabbatical," you should give your worms to a friend to care for.

Fruit Flies

Fruit flies can, on occasion, be a very annoying problem if you keep the worm bins in your house. They will not be present all the time nor in every house at any time but when they are present they are a nuisance. Fruit flies aren't unsanitary, they don't bite or seek out people to bother. They seek out over-ripe fruit and fruit pulp. Usually, fruit flies will hover around the food source that interests them. In high summer we have accepted having a few share our kitchen along with the enormous spread of ripe and ripening tomatoes atop the kitchen counter. When we're making fresh "V-7" juice on demand throughout the day, they tend to congregate over the juicer's discharge pail that holds a mixture of vegetable pulps. If your worm bin contains these types of materials, fruit flies may find it attractive.

Appelhof suggests sucking them up with a vacuum cleaner hose if their numbers become annoying. Fruit flies are a good reason for those of Teutonic tidiness to vermicompost in the basement or outside the house if possible.

Maintenance

After a new bin has been running for a few weeks, you'll see the bedding becoming darker and will spot individual worm casts. Even though food is steadily added, the bedding will gradually vanish. Extensive decomposition of the bedding by other small soil animals and microorganisms begins to be significant.

As worm casts become a larger proportion of the bin, conditions deteriorate for the worms. Eventually the worms suffer and their number and activity begins to drop off. Differences in bedding, temperature, moisture, and the composition of your kitchen's garbage will control how long it takes but eventually you must separate the worms from their castings and put them into fresh bedding. If you're using vermicomposting year-round, it probably will be necessary to regenerate the box about once every four months. There are a number of methods for separating red worms from their castings.

Hand sorting works well after a worm box has first been allowed to run down a bit. The worms are not fed until almost all their food has been consumed and they are living in nearly pure castings. Then lay out a thick sheet of plastic at least four feet square on the ground, floor, or on a table and dump the contents of the worm box on it.

Make six to nine cone-shaped piles. You'll see worms all over. If you're working inside, make sure there is bright light in the room. The worms will move into the center of each pile. Wait five minutes or so and then delicately scrape off the surface of each conical heap, one after another. By the time you finish with the last pile the worms will have retreated further and you can begin with the first heap again.

You repeat this procedure, gradually scraping away casts until there is not much left of the conical heaps. In a surprisingly short time, the worms will all be squirming in the center of a small pile of castings. There is no need to completely separate the worms from all the castings. You can now gather up the worms and place them in fresh bedding to start anew without further inconvenience for another four months. Use the vermicompost on house plants, in the garden, or save it for later.

Hand sorting is particularly useful if you want to give a few pounds of red worms to a friend.

Dividing the box is another, simpler method. You simply remove about two-thirds of the box's contents and spread it on the garden. Then refill the box with fresh bedding and distribute the remaining worms, castings, and food still in the box. Plenty of worms and egg cocoons will remain to populate the box. The worms that you dumped on the garden will probably not survive there.

A better method of dividing a box prevents wasting so many worms. All of the box's contents are pushed to one side, leaving one-third to one-half of the box empty. New bedding and fresh food are put on the "new" side. No food is given to the "old" side for a month or so. By that time virtually all the worms will have migrated to the "new" side. Then the "old" side may be emptied and refilled with fresh bedding.

People in the North may want to use a worm box primarily in winter when other composting methods are inconvenient or impossible. In this case, start feeding the bin heavily from fall through spring and then let it run without much new food until mid-summer. By that time there will be only a few worms left alive in a box of castings. The worms may then be separated from their castings, the box recharged with bedding and the remaining worms can be fed just enough to increase rapidly so that by autumn there will again be enough to eat all your winter garbage.

Garbage Can Composting

Here's a large-capacity vermicomposting system for vegetableatarians and big families. It might even have sufficient digestive capacity for serious juice makers. You'll need two or three, 20 to 30 gallon garbage cans, metal or plastic. In two of them drill numerous half-inch diameter holes from bottom to top and in the lid as well. The third can is used as a tidy way to hold extra dry bedding.

Begin the process with about 10 inches of moist bedding material and worms on the bottom of the first can. Add garbage on top without mixing it in and occasionally sprinkle a thin layer of fresh bedding.

Eventually the first can will be full though it will digest hundreds of gallons of garbage before that happens. When finally full, the bulk of its contents will be finished worm casts and will contain few if any worms. Most of the remaining activity will be on the surface where there is fresh food and more air. Filling the first can may take six months to a year. Then, start the second can by transferring the top few inches of the first, which contains most of the worms, into a few inches of fresh bedding on the bottom of the second can. I'd wait another month for the worms left in the initial can to finish digesting all the remaining garbage. Then, you have 25 to 30 gallons of worm casts ready to be used as compost.

Painting the inside of metal cans with ordinary enamel when they have been emptied will greatly extend their life. Really high-volume kitchens might run two vermicomposting garbage cans at once.

Part II

Composting for The Food Gardener

Chapter 7

Introduction

There is a great deal of confusion in the gardening world about compost, organic matter, humus, fertilizer and their roles in soil fertility, plant health, animal health, human health and gardening success. Some authorities seem to recommend as much manure or compost as possible. Most show inadequate concern about its quality. The slick books published by a major petrochemical corporation correctly acknowledge that soil organic matter is important but give rather vague guidelines as to how much while focusing on chemical fertilizers. Organic gardeners denigrate chemicals as though they were of the devil and like J.I. Rodale in *The Organic Front*, advise:

> *Is it practical to run a garden exclusively with the use of compost, without the aid of so-called chemical or artificial fertilizers? The answer is not only yes, but in such case you will have the finest vegetables obtainable, vegetables fit to grace the table of the most exacting gourmet.*

Since the 1950s a government-funded laboratory at Cornell University has cranked out seriously flawed studies "proving" that food raised with chemicals is just as or even more nutritious than organically grown food. The government's investment in "scientific research" was made to counter unsettling (to various economic interest groups) nutritional and health claims that the organic farming movement had been making. For example, in *The Living Soil*, Lady Eve Balfour observed:

I have lived a healthy country existence practically all my life, and for the last 25 years of it I have been actively engaged in farming. I am physically robust, and have never suffered a major illness, but until 1938 I was seldom free in winter from some form of rheumatism, and from November to April I invariably suffered from a continual succession of head colds. I started making compost by Howard's method using it first on the vegetables for home consumption.... That winter I had no colds at all and almost for the first time in my life was free from rheumatic pains even in prolonged spells of wet weather.

Fifty years later there still exists an intensely polarized dispute about the right way to garden and farm. People who are comfortable disagreeing with Authority and that believe there is a strong connection between soil fertility and the consequent health of plants, animals, and humans living on that soil tend to side with the organic camp. People who consider themselves "practical" or scientific tend to side with the mainstream agronomists and consider chemical agriculture as the only method that can produce enough to permit industrial civilization to exist. For many years I was confused by all this. Have you been too? Or have you taken a position on this controversy and feel that you don't need more information? I once thought the organic camp had all the right answers but years of explaining soil management in gardening books made me reconsider and reconsider again questions like "why is organic matter so important in soil?" and "how much and what kind do we need?" I found these subjects still needed to have clearer answers. This book attempts to provide those answers and puts aside ideology.

A Brief History of the Organic Movement

How did all of this unresolvable controversy begin over something that should be scientifically obvious? About 1900, "experts" increasingly encouraged farmers to use chemical fertilizers and to neglect manuring and composting as unprofitable and unnecessary. At the time this advice seemed practical because chemicals did greatly increase yields and profits while chemistry plus motorized farm machinery minus livestock greatly eased the farmer's workload, allowed the farmer to abandon the production of low-value fodder crops, and concentrate on higher value cash crops.

Perplexing new farming problems—diseases, insects and loss of seed vigor—began appearing after World War 1. These difficulties did not seem obviously connected to industrial agriculture, to abandonment of livestock, manuring, composting, and to dependence on chemistry. The troubled farmers saw themselves as innocent victims of happenstance, needing to hire the chemical plant doctor much as sick people are encouraged by medical doctors to view themselves as victims, who are totally irresponsible for creating their condition and incapable of curing it without costly and dangerous medical intervention.

Farming had been done holistically since before Roman times. Farms inevitably included livestock, and animal manure or compost made with manure or green manures were the main sustainers of soil fertility. In 1900 productive farm soils still contained large reserves of humus from millennia of manuring. As long as humus is present in quantity, small, affordable amounts of chemicals actually do stimulate growth, increase yields, and up profits. And plant health doesn't suffer nor do diseases and insects become plagues. However, humus is not a permanent material and is gradually decomposed. Elimination of manuring steadily reduced humus levels and consequently decreased the life in the soil. And (as will be explained a little later) nitrogen-rich fertilizers accelerate humus loss.

With the decline of organic matter, new problems with plant and animal health gradually developed while insect predation worsened and profits dropped because soils declining in humus need ever larger amounts of fertilizer to maintain yields. These changes developed gradually and erratically, and there was a long lag between the first dependence on chemicals, the resulting soil addiction, and steady increases in farm problems. A new alliance of scientific experts, universities, and agribusiness interests had self-interested reasons to identify other causes than loss of soil humus for the new problems. The increasingly troubled farmer's attention was thus fixated on fighting against plant and animal diseases and insects with newer and better chemicals.

Just as with farm animals, human health also responds to soil fertility. Industrial agriculture steadily lowered the average nutritional quality of food and gradually increased human degeneration, but these effects were masked by a statistical increase in human life span due to improved public sanitation, vaccinations, and, starting in the 1930s, the first antibiotics. As statistics, we were living longer but as individuals, we were feeling poorer. Actually, most of the statistical increase in lifespan is from children that are now surviving childhood diseases. I contend that people who made it to seven years old a century ago had a chance more-or-less equal to ours, of surviving past seventy with a greater probability of feeling good in middle-and old age. People have short memories and tend to think that things always were as they are in the present. Slow but continuous increases in nutritionally related diseases like tooth decay, periodontal disease, diabetes, heart disease, birth defects, mental retardation, drug addiction or cancer are not generally seen as a "new" problem, while subtle reductions in the feeling of well-being go unnoticed.

During the 1930s a number of far-seeing individuals began to worry about the social liabilities from chemically dependent farming. Drs. Robert McCarrison and Weston Price addressed their concerns to other health professionals. Rudolf Steiner, observing that declines in human health were preventing his disciples from achieving spiritual betterment started the gentle biodynamic farming movement. Steiner's principal English speaking followers, Pfeiffer and Koepf, wrote about biological farming and gardening extensively and well.

Professor William Albrecht, Chairman of the Soil Department of the University of Missouri, tried to help farmers raise healthier livestock and made unemotional but very explicit connections between soil fertility, animal, and human health. Any serious gardener or person interested in health and preventive medicine will find the books of all these unique individuals well worth reading.

I doubt that the writings and lectures of any of the above individuals would have sparked a bitter controversy like the intensely ideological struggle that developed between the organic gardening and farming movement and the agribusiness establishment. This was the doing of two energetic and highly puritanical men: Sir Albert Howard and his American disciple, J.I. Rodale.

Howard's criticism was correctly based on observations of improved animal and human health as a result of using compost to build soil fertility. Probably concluding that the average farmer's weak ethical condition would be unable to resist the apparently profitable allures of chemicals unless their moral sense was outraged, Howard undertook an almost religious crusade against the evils of chemical fertilizers. Notice the powerful emotional loading carried in this brief excerpt from Howard's *Soil and Health*:

> *Artificial fertilizers lead to artificial nutrition, artificial animals and finally to artificial men and women.*

Do you want to be "artificial?" Rodale's contentious *Organic Front* makes readers feel morally deficient if they do not agree about the vital importance of recycling organic matter.

> *The Chinese do not use chemical fertilizers. They return to the land every bit of organic matter they can find. In China if you burned over a field or a pile of vegetable rubbish you would be severely punished. There are many fantastic stories as to the lengths the Chinese will go to get human excremental matter. A traveler told me that while he was on the toilet in a Shanghai hotel two men were waiting outside to rush in and make way with the stuff.*

Perhaps you too should be severely punished for wasting your personal organic matter.

Rodale began proselytizing for the organic movement about 1942. With an intensity unique to ideologues, he attacked chemical companies, attacked chemical fertilizers, attacked chemical pesticides, and attacked the scientific agricultural establishment. With a limited technical education behind him, the well-meaning Rodale occasionally made overstatements, wrote oversimplification as science, and uttered scientific absurdities as fact. And he attacked, attacked, attacked all along a broad organic front. So the objects of his attacks defended, defended, defended.

A great deal of confusion was generated from the contradictions between Rodale's self righteous and sometimes scientifically vague positions and the amused defenses of the smug scientific community. Donald Hopkins' *Chemicals, Humus and the Soil* is the best, most humane, and emotionally generous defense against the extremism of Rodale. Hopkins makes hash of many organic principles while still upholding the vital role of humus. Anyone who thinks of themselves as a supporter of organic farming and gardening should first dig up this old, out of print book, and come to terms with Hopkins' arguments.

Organic versus establishment hostilities continued unabated for many years. After his father's death, Rodale's son and heir to the publishing empire, Robert, began to realize that there was a sensible middle ground. However, I suppose Robert Rodale perceived communicating a less ideological message as a problem: most of the readers of *Organic Gardening and Farming* magazine and the buyers of organic gardening books published by Rodale Press weren't open to ambiguity.

I view organic gardeners largely as examples of American Puritanism who want to possess an clear, simple system of capital "T" truth, that brooks no exceptions and has no complications or gray areas. "Organic" as a movement had come to be defined by Rodale publications as growing food by using an approved list of substances that were considered good and virtuous while shunning another list that seemed to be considered "of the devil," similar to kosher and non-kosher food in the orthodox Jewish religion. And like other puritans, the organic faithful could consider themselves superior humans.

But other agricultural reformers have understood that there *are* gray areas—that chemicals are not all bad or all good and that other sane and holistic standards can be applied to decide what is the best way to go about raising crops. These people began to discuss new agricultural methods like Integrated Pest Management (IPM) or Low Input Sustainable Agriculture (LISA), systems that allowed a minimal use of chemistry without abandoning the focus on soil organic matter's vital importance.

My guess is that some years back, Bob Rodale came to see the truth of this, giving him a problem—he did not want to threaten a major source of political and financial support. So he split off the "farming" from *Organic Gardening and Farming* magazine and started two new publications, one called *The New Farm* where safely away from less educated unsophisticated eyes he could discuss minor alterations in the organic faith without upsetting the readers of *Organic Gardening*.

Today's Confusions

I have offered this brief interpretation of the organic gardening and farming movement primarily for the those gardeners who, like me, learned their basics from Rodale Press. Those who do not now cast this heretical book down in disgust but finish it will come away with a broader, more scientific understanding of the vital role of organic matter, some certainty about how much compost you really need to make and use, and the role that both compost and fertilizers can have in creating and maintaining the level of soil fertility needed to grow a great vegetable garden.

Chapter 8

Humus and Soil Productivity

Books about hydroponics sound plausible. That is, until you actually *see* the results. Plants grown in chemical nutrient solutions may be huge but look a little "off." Sickly and weak somehow. Without a living soil, plants can not be totally healthy or grow quite as well as they might.

By focusing on increasing and maximizing soil life instead of adding chemical fertility, organic farmers are able to grow excellent cereals and fodder. On richer soils they can even do this for generations, perhaps even for millennia without bringing in plant nutrients from elsewhere. If little or no product is sent away from the farm, this subsistence approach may be a permanent agricultural system. But even with a healthy ecology few soils are fertile enough by themselves to permit continuous export of their mineral resources by selling crops at market.

Take one step further. Cereals are mostly derived from hardy grasses while other field crops have similar abilities to thrive while being offered relatively low levels of nutrients. With good management, fertile soils are able to present these lower nutritional levels to growing plants without amendment or fortification with potent, concentrated nutrient sources. But most vegetables demand far higher levels of support. Few soils, even fertile soils that have never been farmed, will grow vegetables without improvement. Farmers and gardeners must increase fertility significantly if they want to grow great vegetables. The choices they make while doing this can have a strong effect, not only on their immediate success or failure, but on the actual nutritional quality of the food that they produce.

How Humus Benefits Soil

The roots of plants, soil animals, and most soil microorganisms need to breathe oxygen. Like other oxygen burners, they expel carbon dioxide. For all of them to grow well and be healthy, the earth must remain open, allowing air to enter and leave freely. Otherwise, carbon dioxide builds up to toxic levels. Imagine yourself being suffocated by a plastic bag tied around your neck. It would be about the same thing to a root trying to live in compacted soil.

A soil consisting only of rock particles tends to be airless. A scientist would say it had a high bulk density or lacked pore space. Only coarse sandy soil remains light and open without organic matter. Few soils are formed only of coarse sand, most are mixtures of sand, silt and clay. Sands are sharp-sided, relatively large rock particles similar to table salt or refined white sugar. Irregular edges keep sand particles separated, and allow the free movement of air and moisture.

Silt is formed from sand that has weathered to much smaller sizes, similar to powdered sugar or talcum powder. Through a magnifying lens, the edges of silt particles appear rounded because weak soil acids have actually dissolved them away. A significant amount of the nutrient content of these decomposed rock particles has become plant food or clay. Silt particles can compact tightly, leaving little space for air.

As soil acids break down silts, the less-soluble portions recombine into clay crystals. Clay particles are much smaller than silt grains. It takes an electron microscope to see the flat, layered structures of clay molecules. Shales and slates are rocks formed by heating and compressing clay. Their layered fracture planes mimic the molecules from which they were made. Pure clay is heavy, airless and a very poor medium for plant growth.

Humusless soils that are mixtures of sand, silt, and clay can become extremely compacted and airless because the smaller silt and clay particles sift between the larger sand bits and densely fill all the pore spaces. These soils can also form very hard crusts that resist the infiltration of air, rain, or irrigation water and prevent the emergence of seedlings. Surface crusts form exactly the same way that concrete is finished.

Have you ever seen a finisher screed a concrete slab? First, smooth boards and then, large trowels are run back and forth over liquid concrete. The motion separates the tiny bits of fine sand and cement from denser bits of gravel. The "fines" rise to the surface where they are troweled into a thin smooth skin. The same thing happens when humusless soil is rained on or irrigated with sprinklers emitting a coarse, heavy spray. The droplets beat on the soil, mechanically separating the lighter "fines" (in this case silt and clay) from larger, denser particles. The sand particles sink, the fines rise and dry into a hard, impenetrable crust.

Organic matter decomposing in soil opens and loosens soil and makes the earth far more welcoming to plant growth. Its benefits are both direct and indirect. Decomposing organic matter mechanically acts like springy sponges that reduce compaction. However, rotting is rapid and soon this material and its effect is virtually gone. You can easily create this type of temporary result by tilling a thick dusting of peat moss into some poor soil.

A more significant and longer-lasting soil improvement is created by microorganisms and earthworms, whose activities makes particles of sand, silt, and clay cling strongly together and form large, irregularly-shaped grains called "aggregates" or "crumbs" that resist breaking apart. A well-developed crumb structure gives soil a set of qualities farmers and gardeners delightfully refer to as "good tilth." The difference between good and poor tilth is like night and day to someone working the land. For example, if you rotary till unaggregated soil into a fluffy seedbed, the first time it is irrigated, rained on, or stepped on it slumps back down into an airless mass and probably develops a hard crust as well. However, a soil with good tilth will permit multiple irrigations and a fair amount of foot traffic without compacting or crusting.

Crumbs develop as a result of two similar, interrelated processes. Earthworms and other soil animals make stable humus crumbs as soil, clay and decomposing organic matter pass through their digestive systems. The casts or scats that emerge *are crumbs.* Free-living soil microorganisms also form crumbs. As they eat organic matter they secrete slimes and gums that firmly cement fine soil particles together into long lasting aggregates.

I sadly observe what happens when farmers allow soil organic matter to run down every time I drive in the country. Soil color that should be dark changes to light because mineral particles themselves are usually light colored or reddish; the rich black or chestnut tone soil can get is organic matter. Puddles form when it rains hard on perfectly flat humusless fields and may stand for hours or days, driving out all soil air, drowning earthworms, and suffocating crop roots. On sloping fields the water runs off rather than percolating in. Evidence of this can be seen in muddy streams and in more severe cases, by little rills or mini-gullies across the field caused by fast moving water sweeping up soil particles from the crusted surface as it leaves the field.

Later, the farmers will complain of drought or infertility and seek to support their crops with irrigation and chemicals. Actually, if all the water that had fallen on the field had percolated into the earth, the crops probably would not have suffered at all even from extended spells without rain. These same humusless fields lose a lot more soil in the form of blowing dust clouds when tilled in a dryish state.

The greatest part of farm soil erosion is caused by failing to maintain necessary levels of humus. As a nation, America is losing its best cropland at a unsustainable rate. No civilization in history has yet survived the loss of its prime farmland. Before industrial technology placed thousands of times more force into the hands of the farmer, humans still managed to make an impoverished semi-desert out of every civilized region within 1,000–1,500 years. This sad story is told in Carter and Dale's fascinating, but disturbing, book called *Topsoil and Civilization* that I believe should be read by every thoughtful person. Unless we significantly alter our "improved" farming methods we will probably do the same to America in another century or two.

The Earthworm's Role in Soil Fertility

Soil fertility has been gauged by different measures. Howard repeatedly insisted that the only good yardstick was humus content. Others are so impressed by the earthworm's essential functions that they count worms per acre and say that this number measures soil fertility. The two standards of evaluation are closely related.

When active, some species of earthworms daily eat a quantity of soil equal to their own body weight. After passing through the worm's gut, this soil has been chemically altered. Minerals, especially phosphorus which tends to be locked up as insoluble calcium phosphate and consequently unavailable to plants, become soluble in the worm's gut, and thus available to nourish growing plants. And nitrogen held in organic matter is altered to soluble nitrate nitrogen. In fact, compared to the surrounding soil, worm casts are five times as rich in nitrate nitrogen; twice as rich in soluble calcium; contain two and one-half times as much available magnesium; are seven times as rich in available phosphorus, and offer plants eleven times as much potassium. Earthworms are equally capable of making trace minerals available.

Highly fertile earthworm casts can amount to a large proportion of the entire soil mass. When soil is damp and cool enough to encourage earthworm activity, an average of 700 pounds of worm casts per acre are produced each day. Over a year's time in the humid eastern United States, 100,000 pounds of highly fertile casts per acre may be generated. Imagine! That's like 50 tons of low-grade fertilizer per acre per year containing more readily available NPK, Ca, Mg and so forth, than farmers apply to grow cereal crops like wheat, corn, or soybeans. A level of fertility that will grow wheat is not enough nutrition to grow vegetables, but earthworms can make a major contribution to the garden.

At age 28, Charles Darwin presented "On the Formation of Mould" to the Geological Society of London. This lecture illustrated the amazing churning effect of the earthworm on soil. Darwin observed some chunks of lime that had been left on the surface of a meadow. A few years later they were found several inches below the surface. Darwin said this was the work of earthworms, depositing castings that "sooner or later spread out and cover any object left on the surface." In a later book, Darwin said:

> The plow is one of the most ancient and most valuable of man's inventions; but long before he existed the land was in fact regularly plowed and still continues to be thus plowed by earthworms. It may be doubted whether there are many other animals which have played so important a part in the history of the world, as have these lowly organized creatures.

Earthworms also prevent runoff. They increase percolation of water into fine-textured soils by making a complex system of interconnected channels or tunnels throughout the topsoil. In one study, soil lacking worms had an absorption rate of 0.2 inches of rainfall per minute. Earthworms were added and allowed to work over that soil sample for one month. Then, infiltration rates increased to 0.9 inches of rainfall per minute. Much of what we know about earthworms is due to Dr. Henry Hopp who worked for the United States Department of Agriculture during the 1940s. Dr. Hopp's interesting booklet, *What Every Gardener Should Know About Earthworms.* is still in print. In one Hopp research project, some very run-down clay soil was placed in six large flowerpots. Nothing was done to a pair of control pots, fertilizer was blended in and grass sod grown on two others, while mulch was spread over two more. Then worms were added to one of each pair of pots. In short order all of the worms added to the unimproved pot were dead. There was nothing in that soil to feed them. The sod alone increased percolation but where

Percolation rate in inches per minute

Amendment to clay soil	Without worms	With worms
None	0.0	0.0
Grass & fertilizer	0.1	0.8
Mulch	0.0	1.5

the sod or mulch fed a worm population, infiltration of water was far better.

Most people who honestly consider these facts conclude that the earthworm's activities are a major factor in soil productivity. Study after scientific study has shown that the quality and yield of pastures is directly related to their earthworm count. So it seems only reasonable to evaluate soil management practices by their effect on earthworm counts.

Earthworm populations will vary enormously according to climate and native soil fertility. Earthworms need moisture; few if any will be found in deserts. Highly mineralized soils that produce a lot of biomass will naturally have more worms than infertile soils lacking humus. Dr. Hopp surveyed worm populations in various farm soils. The table below shows what a gardener might expect to find in their own garden by contrasting samples from rich and poor soils. The data also suggest a guideline for how high worm populations might be usefully increased by adding organic matter. The worms were counted at their seasonal population peak by carefully examining a section of soil exactly one foot square by seven inches deep. If you plan to take a census in your own garden, keep in mind that earthworm counts will be highest in spring.

Earthworms are inhibited by acid soils and/or soils deficient in calcium. Far larger populations of worms live in soils that weathered out of underlying limestone rocks. In one experiment, earthworm counts in a pasture went up from 51,000 per acre in acid soil to 441,000 per acre two years after lime and a non-acidifying chemical fertilizer was spread. Rodale and Howard loudly and repeatedly contended that chemical fertilizers decimate earthworm populations. Swept up in what I view as a self-righteous crusade against chemical agriculture, they included all fertilizers in this category for tactical reasons.

Howard especially denigrated sulfate of ammonia and single super-phosphate as earthworm poisons. Both of these chemical fertilizers are made with sulfuric acid and have a powerful acidifying reaction when they dissolve in soil. Rodale correctly pointed out that golf course groundskeepers use repeated applications of ammonium sulfate to eliminate earthworms from putting greens. (Small mounds of worm

Location	Worms per sq. ft.	Worms per acre
Marcellus, NY	38	1,600,000
Ithica, NY	4	190,000
Frederick, MD	50	2,200,000
Beltsville, MD	8	350,000
Zanesville, OH	37	1,600,000
Coshocton, OH	5	220,000
Mayaquez, P.R.[1]	6	260,000

casts made by nightcrawlers ruin the greens' perfectly smooth surface so these worms are the bane of greenskeepers.) However, ammonium sulfate does not eliminate or reduce worms when the soil contains large amounts of chalk or other forms of calcium that counteract acidity.

The truth of the matter is that worms eat decaying organic matter and any soil amendment that increases plant growth without acidifying soil will increase earthworm food supply and thus worm population. Using lime as an antidote to acid-based fertilizers prevents making the soil inhospitable to earthworms. And many chemical fertilizers do not provoke acid reactions. The organic movement loses this round-but not the battle. And certainly not the war.

Food supply primarily determines earthworm population. To increase their numbers it is merely necessary to bring in additional organic matter or add plant nutrients that cause more vegetation to be grown there. In one study, simply returning the manure resulting from hay taken off a pasture increased earthworms by one-third. Adding lime and superphosphate to that manure made an additional improvement of another 33 percent. Every time compost is added to a garden, the soil's ability to support earthworms increases.

Some overly enthusiastic worm fanciers believe it is useful to import large numbers of earthworms. I do not agree. These same self-interested

---

[1] Because of the high rate of bacterial decomposition, few earthworms are found in tropical soils unless they are continuously amended with substantial quantities of organic matter.

individuals tend to breed and sell worms. If the variety being offered is *Eisenia foetida,* the brandling, red wiggler, or manure worm used in vermicomposting, adding them to soil is a complete waste of money. This species does not survive well in ordinary soil and can breed in large numbers only in decomposing manure or other proteinaceous organic waste with a low C/N. All worm species breed prolifically. If there are *any* desirable worms present in soil, their population will soon match the available food supply and soil conditions. The way to increase worm populations is to increase organic matter, up mineral fertility, and eliminate acidity.

Earthworms and their beneficial activities are easily overlooked and left out of our contemplations on proper gardening technique. But understanding their breeding cycle allows gardeners to easily assist the worms efforts to multiply. In temperate climates, young earthworms hatch out in the fall when soil is cooling and moisture levels are high. As long as the soil is not too cold they feed actively and grow. By early spring these young worms are busily laying eggs. With summer's heat the soil warms and dries out. Even if the gardener irrigates, earthworms naturally become less active. They still lay a few eggs but many mature worms die. During high summer the few earthworms found will be small and young. Unhatched eggs are plentiful but not readily noticed by casual inspection so gardeners may mistakenly think they have few worms and may worry about how to increase their populations. With autumn the population cycle begins anew.

Soil management can greatly alter worm populations. But, how the field is handled during summer has only a slight effect. Spring and summer tillage does kill a few worms but does not damage eggs. By mulching, the soil can be kept cooler and more favorable to worm activities during summer while surface layers are kept moister. Irrigation helps similarly. Doing these things will allow a gardener the dubious satisfaction of seeing a few more worms during the main gardening season. However, soil is supposed to become inhospitably hot and dry during summer (worm's eye view) and there's not much point in struggling to maintain large earthworm populations during that part of the year. Unfortunately, summer is when gardeners pay the closest attention to the soil.

Worms maintain their year-round population by overwintering and then laying eggs that hatch late in the growing season. The most harm to worm multiplication happens by exposing bare soil during winter. Worm activity should be at a peak during cool weather. Though worms inadvertently pass a lot of soil through their bodies as they tunnel, soil is not their food. Garden worms and nightcrawlers intentionally rise to the surface to feed. They consume decaying vegetation lying on the surface. Without this food supply they die off. And in northern winters worms must be protected from suddenly experiencing freezing temperatures while they "harden off" and adapt themselves to surviving in almost frozen soil. Under sod or where protected by insulating mulch or a layer of organic debris, soil temperature drops gradually as winter comes on. But the first day or two of cold winter weather may freeze bare soil solid and kill off an entire field full of worms before they've had a chance to adapt.

Almost any kind of ground cover will enhance winter survival. A layer of compost, manure, straw, or a well-grown cover crop of ryegrass, even a thin mulch of grass clippings or weeds can serve as the food source worms need. Dr. Hopp says that soil tilth can be improved a great deal merely by assisting worms over a single winter.

Gardeners can effectively support the common earthworm without making great alterations in the way we handle our soil. From a worm's viewpoint, perhaps the best way to recycle autumn leaves is to till them in very *shallowly* over the garden so they serve as insulation yet are mixed with enough soil so that decomposition is accelerated. Perhaps a thorough garden clean-up is best postponed until spring, leaving a significant amount of decaying vegetation on top of the soil. (Of course, you'll want to remove and compost any diseased plant material or species that may harbor overwintering pests.) The best time to apply compost to tilled soil may also be during the autumn and the very best way is as a dressing atop a leaf mulch because the compost will also accelerate leaf decomposition. This is called "sheet composting" and will be discussed in detail shortly.

Certain pesticides approved for general use can severely damage earthworms. Carbaryl (Sevin), one of the most commonly used home garden chemical pesticides, is deadly to earthworms even at low levels. Malathion is moderately toxic to worms. Diazinon has not been shown to be at all harmful to earthworms when used at normal rates.

Just because a pesticide is derived from a natural source and is approved for use on crops labeled "organically grown" is no guarantee that it is not poisonous to mammals or highly toxic to earthworms. For example, rotenone, an insecticide derived from a tropical root called derris, is as poisonous to humans as organophosphate chemical pesticides. Even in very dilute amounts, rotenone is highly toxic to fish and other aquatic life. Great care must be taken to prevent it from getting into waterways. In the tropics, people traditionally harvest great quantities of fish by tossing a handful of powdered derris (a root containing rotenone) into the water, waiting a few minutes, and then scooping up stunned, dead, and dying fish by the ton. Rotenone is also deadly to earthworms. However, rotenone rarely kills worms because it is so rapidly biodegradable. Sprayed on plants to control beetles and other plant predators, its powerful effect lasts only a day or so before sun and moisture break it down to harmless substances. But once I dusted an entire raised bed of beetle-threatened bush bean seedlings with powdered rotenone late in the afternoon. The spotted beetles making hash of their leaves were immediately killed. Unexpectedly, it rained rather hard that evening and still-active rotenone was washed off the leaves and deeply into the soil. The next morning the surface of the bed was thickly littered with dead earthworms. I've learned to treat rotenone with great caution.

Microbes and Soil Fertility

There are still other holistic standards to measure soil productivity. With more than adequate justification the great Russian soil microbiologist

N.S. Krasilnikov judged fertility by counting the numbers of microbes present. He said:

> *...soil fertility is determined by biological factors, mainly by microorganisms. The development of life in soil endows it with the property of fertility. The notion of soil is inseparable from the notion of the development of living organisms in it. Soil is created by microorganisms. Were this life dead or stopped, the former soil would become an object of geology [not biology].*

Louise Howard, Sir Albert's second wife, made a very similar judgment in her book, *Sir Albert Howard in India.*

> *A fertile soil, that is, a soil teeming with healthy life in the shape of abundant microflora and microfauna, will bear healthy plants, and these, when consumed by animals and man, will confer health on animals and man. But an infertile soil, that is, one lacking in sufficient microbial, fungous, and other life, will pass on some form of deficiency to the plants, and such plant, in turn, who pass on some form of deficiency to animal and man.*

Although the two quotes substantively agree, Krasilnikov had a broader understanding. The early writers of the organic movement focused intently on mycorrhizal associations between soil fungi and plant roots as *the* hidden secret of plant health. Krasilnikov, whose later writings benefited from massive Soviet research did not deny the significance of mycorrhizal associations but stressed plant-bacterial associations. Both views contain much truth.

Krasilnikov may well have been the greatest soil microbiologist of his era, and Russians in general seem far ahead of us in this field. It is worth taking a moment to ask why that is so. American agricultural science is motivated by agribusiness, either by direct subsidy or indirectly through government because our government is often strongly influenced by major economic interests. American agricultural research also exists in a relatively free market where at this moment in history, large quantities of manufactured materials are reliably and cheaply available. Western agricultural science thus tends to seek solutions involving manufactured inputs. After all, what good is a problem if you can't solve it by profitably selling something .

But any Soviet agricultural researcher who solved problems by using factory products would be dooming their farmers to failure because the U.S.S.R.'s economic system was incapable of regularly supplying such items. So logically, Soviet agronomy focused on more holistic, low-tech approaches such as manipulating the soil microecology. For example, Americans scientifically increase soil nitrogen by spreading industrial chemicals; the Russians found low-tech ways to brew bacterial soups that inoculated a field with slightly more efficient nitrogen fixing microorganisms.

Soil microbiology is also a relatively inexpensive line of research that rewards mental cleverness over massive investment. Multimillion dollar laboratories with high-tech equipment did not yield big answers when the study was new. Perhaps in this biotech era, recombinant genetics will find high-tech ways to tailor make improved microorganisms and we'll surpass the Russians.

Soil microorganism populations are incredibly high. In productive soils there may be billions to the gram. (One gram of fluffy soil might fill 1/2 teaspoon.) Krasilnikov found great variations in bacterial counts. Light-colored nonproductive earths of the North growing skimpy conifer trees or poor crops don't contain very many microorganisms. The rich, black, grain-producing soils of the Ukraine (like our midwestern corn belt) carry very large microbial populations.

One must be clever to study soil microbes and fungi. Their life processes and ecological interactions can't be easily observed directly in the soil with a microscope. Usually, scientists study microorganisms by finding an artificial medium on which they grow well and observe the activities of a large colony or pure culture—a very restricted view. There probably are more species of microorganisms than all other living things combined, yet we often can't identify one species from another similar one by their appearance. We can generally classify bacteria by shape: round ones, rod-shaped ones, spiral ones, etc. We differentiate them by which antibiotic kills them and by which variety of artificial material they prefer to grow on. Pathogens are recognized by their prey. Still, most microbial activities remain a great mystery.

Krasilnikov's great contribution to science was discovering how soil microorganisms assist the growth of higher plants. Bacteria are very fussy about the substrate they'll grow on. In the laboratory, one species grows on protein gel, another on seaweed. One thrives on beet pulp while another only grows on a certain cereal extract. Plants "understand" this and manipulate their soil environment to enhance the reproduction of certain bacteria they find desirable while suppressing others. This is accomplished by root exudates.

For every 100 grams of above-ground biomass, a plant will excrete about 25 grams of root exudates, creating a chemically different zone (rhizosphere) close to the root that functions much like the culture medium in a laboratory. Certain bacteria find this region highly favorable and multiply prolifically, others are suppressed. Bacterial counts adjacent to roots will be in hundreds of millions to billions per gram of soil. A fraction of an inch away beyond the influence of the exudates, the count drops greatly.

Why do plants expend energy culturing bacteria? Because there is an exchange, a *quid pro quo*. These same bacteria assist the plant in numerous ways. Certain types of microbes are predators. Instead of consuming dead organic matter they attack living plants. However, other species, especially actinomycetes, give off antibiotics that suppress pathogens. The multiplication of actinomycetes can be enhanced by root exudates.

Perhaps the most important benefit plants receive from soil bacteria are what Krasilnikov dubbed "phytamins," a word play on vitamins plus *phyta* or "plant" in Greek. Helpful bacteria exude complex water-soluble organic molecules that plants uptake through their roots and use much like humans need certain vitamins. When plants are deprived of phytamins they are less than optimally healthy, have lowered disease resistance, and may not grow as large because some phytamins act as growth hormones.

Keep in mind that beneficial microorganisms clustering around plant roots do not primarily eat root exudates; exudates merely optimize environmental conditions to encourage certain species. The main food of these soil organisms is decaying organic matter and humus. Deficiencies in organic matter or soil pH outside a comfortable range of 5.75–7.5 greatly inhibit beneficial microorganisms.

For a long time it has been standard "chemical" ag science to deride the notion that plant roots can absorb anything larger than simple, inorganic molecules in water solution. This insupportable view is no longer politically correct even among adherents of chemical usage. However, if you should ever encounter an "expert" still trying to intimidate others with these old arguments merely ask them, since plant roots cannot assimilate large organic molecules, why do people succeed using systemic chemical pesticides? Systemics are large, complex poisonous organic molecules that plants uptake through their roots and that then make the above-ground plant material toxic to predators. Ornamentals, like roses, are frequently protected by systemic chemical pesticides mixed into chemical fertilizer and fed through the soil.

Root exudates have numerous functions beyond affecting microorganisms. One is to suppress or encourage the growth of surrounding plants Gardeners experience this as plant companions and antagonists. Walnut tree root exudates are very antagonistic to many other species. And members of the onion family prevent beans from growing well if their root systems are intermixed.

Many crop rotational schemes exist because the effects of root exudates seem to persist for one or even two years after the original plant grew That's why onions grow very well when they are planted where potatoes grew the year before. And why farmers grow a three year rotation of hay, potatoes and onions. That is also why onions don't grow nearly as well following cabbage or squash. Farmers have a much easier time managing successions. They can grow 40 acres of one crop followed by 40 acres of another. But squash from 100 square feet may overwhelm the kitchen while carrots from the same 100 square feet the next year may not be enough. Unless you keep detailed records, it is hard to remember exactly where everything grew as long as two years ago in a vegetable garden and to correlate that data with this year's results. But when I see half a planting on a raised bed grow well and the adjacent half grow poorly, I assume the difficulty was caused by exudate remains from whatever grew there one, or even, two years ago.

In 1990, half of crop "F" grew well, half poorly. this was due to the presence of crop "D" in 1989. The gardener might remember that "D" was there last year. But in 1991, half of crop "G" grew well, half poorly. This was also due to the presence of crop "D" two years ago. Few can make this association.

These effects were one reason that Sir Albert Howard thought it was very foolish to grow a vegetable garden in one spot for too many years. He recommended growing "healing grass" for about five years following several years of vegetable gardening to erase all the exudate effects and restore the soil ecology to normal.

Mycorrhizal association is another beneficial relationship that should exist between soil organisms and many higher plants. This symbiotic relationship involves fungi and plant roots. Fungi can be pathogenic, consuming living plants. But most of them are harmless and eat only dead, decaying organic matter. Most fungi are soil dwellers though some eat downed or even standing trees.

Most people do not realize that plant roots adsorb water and water-soluble nutrients only through the tiny hairs and actively growing tips near the very end of the root. The ability for any new root to absorb nutrition only lasts a short time, then the hairs slough off and the root develops a sort of hard bark. If root system growth slows or stops, the plant's ability to obtain nourishment is greatly reduced. Roots cannot make oxygen out of carbon dioxide as do the leaves. That's why it is so important to maintain a good supply of soil air and for the soil to remain loose enough to allow rapid root expansion.

When roots are cramped, top growth slows or ceases, health and disease resistance drops, and plants may become stressed despite applications of nutrients or watering. Other plants that do not seem to be competing for light above ground may have ramified (filled with roots) far wider expanses soil than a person might think. Once soil is saturated with the roots and the exudates from one plant, the same space may be closed off to the roots of another. Gardeners who use close plantings and intensive raised beds often unknowingly bump up against this limiting factor and are disappointed at the small size of their vegetables despite heavy fertilization, despite loosening the earth two feet deep with double digging, and despite regular watering. Thought about in this way, it should be obvious why double digging improves growth on crowded beds by increasing the depth to which plants can root.

The roots of plants have no way to aggressively breakdown rock particles or organic matter, nor to sort out one nutrient from another. They uptake everything that is in solution, no more, no less while replacing water evaporated from their leaves. However, soil fungi are able to aggressively attack organic matter and even mineral rock particles and extract the nutrition they want. Fungi live in soil as long, complexly interconnected hair-like threads usually only one cell thick. The threads are called "hyphae." Food circulates throughout the hyphae much like blood in a human body. Sometimes, individual fungi can grow to enormous sizes; there are mushroom circles hundreds of feet in diameter that essentially are one single very old organism. The mushrooms we think of when we think "fungus" are actually not the organism, but the transitory fruit of a large, below ground network.

Certain types of fungi are able to form a symbiosis with specific plant species. They insert a hyphae into the gap between individual plant cells in a root hair or just behind the growing root tip. Then the hyphae "drinks" from the vascular system of the plant, robbing it of a bit of its life's blood. However, this is not harmful predation because as the root grows, a bark develops around the hyphae. The bark pinches off the hyphae and it rapidly decays inside the plant, making a contribution of nutrients that the plant couldn't otherwise obtain. Hyphae breakdown products may be in the form of complex organic molecules that function as phytamins for the plant.

Not all plants are capable of forming mycorrhizal associations. Members of the cabbage family, for example, do not. However, if the species can benefit from such an association and does not have one, then despite fertilization the plant will not be as healthy as it could be, nor grow as well. This phenomenon is commonly seen in conifer tree nurseries where seedling beds are first completely sterilized with harsh chemicals and then tree seeds sown. Although thoroughly fertilized, the tiny trees grow slowly for a year or so. Then, as spores of mycorrhizal fungi begin falling on the bed and their hyphae become established, scattered trees begin to develop the necessary symbiosis and their growth takes off. On a bed of two-year-old seedlings, many individual trees are head and shoulders above the others. This is not due to superior genetics or erratic soil fertility. These are the individuals with a mycorrhizal association.

Like other beneficial microorganisms, mycorrhizal fungi do not primarily eat plant vascular fluid, their food is decaying organic matter. Here's yet another reason to contend that soil productivity can be measured by humus content.

Chapter 9

Maintaining Soil Humus

Organic matter benefits soil productivity not because it is present, but because all forms of organic matter in the soil, including its most stable form—humus—are disappearing. Mycorrhizal fungi and beneficial bacterial colonies around plant roots can exist only by consuming soil organic matter. The slimes and gums that cement soil particles into relatively stable aggregates are formed by microorganisms as they consume soil organic matter. Scats and casts that *are* soil crumbs form only because organic matter is being consumed. If humus declines, the entire soil ecology runs down and with it, soil tilth and the health and productivity of plants.

If you want to manage your garden soil wisely, keep foremost in mind that the rate of humus loss is far more important than the amount of humus present. However, natural processes remove humus without our aid or attention while the gardener's task is to add organic matter. So there is a very understandable tendency to focus on addition, not subtraction. But, can we add too much? And if so, what happens when we do?

How Much Humus is Soil Supposed to Have?

If you measured the organic matter contents of various soils around the United States there would be wide differences. Some variations on crop land are due to great losses that have been caused by mismanagement. But even if you could measure virgin soils never used by humans there still would be great differences. Hans Jenny, a soil scientist at the

University of Missouri during the 1940s, noticed patterns in soil humus levels and explained how and why this occurs in a wonderfully readable book, *Factors in Soil Formation*. These days, academic agricultural scientists conceal the basic simplicity of their knowledge by unnecessarily expressing their data with exotic verbiage and higher mathematics. In Jenny's time it was not considered demeaning if an intelligent layman could read and understand the writings of a scientist or scholar. Any serious gardener who wants to understand the wide differences in soil should become familiar with *Factors in Soil Formation*. About organic matter in virgin soils, Jenny said:

> *Within regions of similar moisture conditions, the organic matter content of soil ... decreases from north to south. For each fall of 10° C (18° F) in annual temperature the average organic matter content of soil increases two or three times, provided that [soil moisture] is kept constant.*

Moist soil during the growing season encourages plant growth and thus organic matter production. Where the soil becomes dry during the growing season, plant growth slows or stops.

So, all things being equal, wet soils contain more organic matter than dry ones. All organic matter eventually rots, even in soil too dry to grow plants. The higher the soil temperature the faster the decomposition. But chilly (not frozen) soils can still grow a lot of biomass. So, all things being equal, hot soils have less humus in them than cold ones. Cool, wet soils will have the highest levels; hot, dry soils will be lowest in humus.

This model checks out in practice. If we were to measure organic matter in soils along the Mississippi River where soil moisture conditions remain pretty similar from south to north, we might find 2 percent in sultry Arkansas, 3 percent in Missouri and over 4 percent in Wisconsin, where soil temperatures are much lower. In Arizona, unirrigated desert soils have virtually no organic matter. In central and southern California where skimpy and undependable winter rains peter out by March, it is hard to find an unirrigated soil containing as much as 1 percent organic matter while in the cool Maritime northwest, reliable winter rains keep the soil damp into June and the more fertile farm pastures or natural prairies may develop as much as 5 percent organic matter.

Other factors, like the basic mineral content of the soil or its texture, also influence the amount of organic matter a spot will create and will somewhat increase or decrease the humus content compared to neighboring locations experiencing the same climate. But the most powerfully controlling influences are moisture and temperature.

On all virgin soils the organic matter content naturally sustains itself at the highest possible level. And, average annual additions exactly match the average annual amount of decomposition. Think about that for a moment. Imagine that we start out with a plot of finely-ground rock particles containing no life and no organic matter. As the rock dust is colonized by life forms that gradually build in numbers it becomes soil. The organic matter created there increases nutrient availability and accelerates the breakdown of rock particles, further increasing the creation of organic matter. Soil humus steadily increases. Eventually a climax is sustained where there is as much humus in the soil as there can be.

The peak plant and soil ecology that naturally lives on any site is usually very healthy and is inevitably just as abundant as there is moisture and soil minerals to support it. To me this suggests how much organic matter it takes to grow a great vegetable garden. My theory is that in terms of soil organic matter, vegetables grow quite well at the humus level that would peak naturally on a virgin site. In semi-arid areas I'd modify the theory to include an increase as a result of necessary irrigation. Expressed as a rough rule of thumb, a mere 2 percent organic matter in hot climates increasing to 5 percent in cool ones will supply sufficient biological soil activities to grow healthy vegetables if *the mineral nutrient levels are high enough too.*

Recall my assertion that what is most important about organic matter is not how much is present, but how much is lost each year through decomposition. For only by decomposing does organic matter release the nutrients it contains so plants can uptake them; only by being consumed does humus support the microecology that so markedly contributes phytamins to plant nutrition, aggressively breaks down rock particles and releases the plant nutrients they contain; only by being eaten does soil organic matter support bacteria and earthworms that improve productivity and create better tilth.

Here's something I find very interesting. Temperate climates having seasons and winter, vary greatly in average temperature. Comparing annual decomposition loss from a hot soil carrying 2 percent humus with annual decomposition loss from a cooler soil carrying 5 percent, roughly the same amount of organic matter will decay out of each soil during the growing season. *This means that in temperate regions we have to replace about the same amount of organic matter no matter what the location.*

Like other substantial colleges of agriculture, the University of Missouri ran some very valuable long-term studies in soil management. In 1888, a never-farmed field of native prairie grasses was converted into test plots. For fifty succeeding years each plot was managed in a different but consistent manner. The series of experiments that I find the most helpful recorded what happens to soil organic matter as a consequence of farming practices. The virgin prairie had sustained an organic matter content of about 3.5 percent. The lines on the graph show what happened to that organic matter over time.

Timothy grass is probably a slightly more efficient converter of solar energy into organic matter than was the original prairie. After fifty years of feeding the hay cut from the field and returning all of the livestock's manure, the organic matter in the soil increased about 0.5 percent. Obviously, green manuring has very limited ability to increase soil humus above climax levels. Growing oats and returning enough manure to represent the straw and grain fed to livestock, the field held its organic matter relatively constant.

Growing small grain and removing everything but the stubble for fifty years greatly reduced the organic matter. Keep in mind that half the biomass production in a field happens below ground as roots. And keep in mind that the charts don't reveal the sad appearance the crops

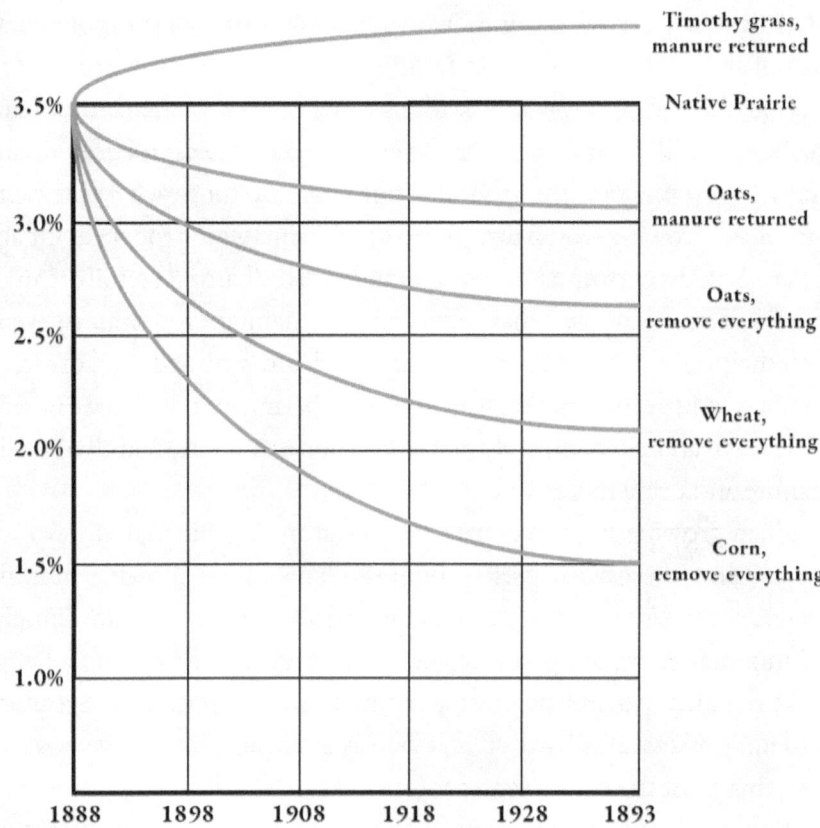

probably had once the organic matter declined significantly. Nor do they show that the seed produced on those degenerated fields probably would no longer sprout well enough to be used as seed grain, so new seed would have been imported into the system each season, bringing with it new supplies of plant nutrients. Without importing that bushel or so of wheat seed on each acre each year, the curves would have been steeper and gone even lower.

Corn is the hardest of the cereals on soil humus. The reason is, wheat is closely broadcast in fall and makes a thick grassy overwintering stand that forms biomass out of most of the solar energy striking the field from spring until early summer when the seed forms. Leafy oats create a little more biomass than wheat. Corn, on the other hand, is frost tender and can't be planted early. It is also not closely planted but is sown in widely-spaced rows. Corn takes quite a while before it forms a leaf canopy that uses all available solar energy. In farming lingo, corn is a "row crop."

Vegetables are also row crops. Many types don't form dense canopies that soak up all solar energy for the entire growing season like a virgin prairie. As with corn, the ground is tilled bare, so for much of the best part of the growing season little or no organic matter is produced. Of all the crops that a person can grow, vegetables are the hardest on soil organic matter. There is no way that vegetables can maintain soil humus, even if all their residues are religiously composted and returned. Soil organic matter would decline markedly even in an experiment in which we raised some small animals exclusively on the vegetables and returned all of their manure and urine too.

When growing vegetables we have to restore organic matter beyond the amount the garden itself produces. The curves showing humus decline at the University of Missouri give us a good hint as to how much organic matter we are going to lose from vegetable gardening. Let's make the most pessimistic possible estimate and suppose that vegetable gardening is twice as hard on soil as was growing corn and removing everything but the stubble and root systems.

With corn, about 40 percent of the entire organic matter reserve is depleted in the first ten years. Let's suppose that vegetables might remove almost *all* soil humus in ten years, or 10 percent each year for the first few years. This number is a crude. and for most places in America, a wildly pessimistic guess.

However, 10 percent loss per year may understate losses in some places. I have seen old row crop soils in California's central valley that look like white-colored blowing dust. Nor does a 10 percent per year estimate quite allow for the surprising durability I observe in the still black and rich-looking old vegetable seed fields of western Washington State's Skaget Valley. These cool climate fields have suffered chemical farming for decades without having been completely destroyed—yet.

How much loss is 10 percent per year? Let's take my own garden for example. It started out as an old hay pasture that hadn't seen a plow for twenty-five or more years and where, for the five years I've owned the property, the annual grass production is not cut, baled, and sold but is cut and allowed to lie in place. Each year's accumulation of minerals and humus contributes to the better growth of the next year's grass. Initially, my grass had grown a little higher and a little thicker each year. But the steady increase in biomass production seems to have tapered off in the last couple of years. I suppose by now the soil's organic matter content probably has been restored and is about 5 percent.

I allocate about one acre of that old pasture to garden land. In any given year my shifting gardens occupy one-third of that acre. The other two-thirds are being regenerated in healing grass. I measure my garden in fractions of acres. Most city folks have little concept of an acre; its about 40,000 square feet, or a plot 200' x 200'.

Give or take some, the plow pan of an acre weighs about two million pounds. The plow pan is that seven inches of topsoil that is flipped over by a moldboard plow, the seven inches where most biological activity occurs, where virtually all of the soil's organic matter resides. Two million pounds equals one thousand tons of topsoil in the first seven inches of an acre. Five percent of that one thousand tons can be organic matter, up to fifty priceless tons of life that changes 950 tons of dead dust into a fertile, productive acre. If 10 percent of that fifty tons is lost as a consequence of one year's vegetable gardening, that amounts to five tons per acre per year lost or about 25 pounds lost per 100 square feet.

Patience, reader. There is a very blunt and soon to be a very obvious point to all of this arithmetic. Visualize this! Lime is spread at rates up to four tons per acre. Have you ever spread 1 T/A or 50 pounds of lime over a garden 33 x 33 feet? Mighty hard to accomplish! Even 200 pounds of lime would barely whiten the ground of a 1,000 square-foot garden. It is even harder to spread a mere 5 tons of compost over an acre or only 25 pounds on a 100-square-foot bed. It seems as though nothing has been accomplished, most of the soil still shows, there is no *layer* of compost, only a thin scattering.

But for the purpose of maintaining humus content of vegetable ground at a healthy level, a thin scattering once a year is a gracious plenty. Even if I were starting with a totally depleted, dusty, absolutely humusless, ruined old farm field that had no organic matter whatsoever and I wanted to convert it to a healthy vegetable garden, I would only have to make a one-time amendment of 50 tons of ripe compost per acre or 2,500 pounds per 1,000 square feet. Now 2,500 pounds of humus is a groaning, spring-sagging, long-bed pickup load of compost heaped up above the cab and dripping off the sides. Spread on a small garden, that's enough to feel a sense of accomplishment about. Before I knew better I used to incorporate that much composted horse manure once or twice a year and when I did add a half-inch thick layer that's about what I was applying.

Fertilizing Vegetables with Compost

Will a five ton per acre addition of compost provide enough nutrition to grow great vegetables? Unfortunately, the answer usually is no. In most gardens, in most climates, with most of what passes for "compost," it probably won't. That much compost might well grow decent wheat.

The factors involved in making this statement are numerous and too complex to fully analyze in a little book like this one. They include the intrinsic mineralization of the soil itself, the temperature of the soil during the growing season, and the high nutritional needs of the vegetables themselves. In my experience, a few alluvial soils that get regular, small additions of organic matter can grow good vegetable crops without additional help. However, these sites are regularly flooded and replenished with highly mineralized rock particles. Additionally, they must become very warm during the growing season. But not all rock particles contain high levels of plant nutrients and not all soils get hot enough to rapidly break down soil particles.

Soil temperature has a great deal to do with how effectively compost can act as fertilizer. Sandy soils warm up much faster in spring and sand allows for a much freer movement of air, so humus decomposes much more rapidly in sand. Perhaps a sunny, sandy garden on a south-facing slope might grow pretty well with small amounts of strong compost. As a practical matter, if most people spread even the most potent compost over their gardens at only twenty-five pounds per 100 square feet, they would almost certainly be disappointed.

Well then, if five tons of quality compost to the acre isn't adequate for most vegetables, what about using ten or twenty tons of the best. Will that grow a good garden? Again, the answer must allow for a lot of factors but is generally more positive. If the compost has a low C/N and that compost, or the soil itself, isn't grossly deficient in some essential nutrient, and if the soil has a coarse, airy texture that promotes decomposition, then somewhat heavier applications will grow a good-looking garden that yields a lot of food.

However, one question that is rarely asked and even more rarely answered satisfactorily in the holistic farming and gardening lore is: Precisely how much organic matter or humus is needed to maximize plant health and the nutritional qualities of the food we're growing? An almost equally important corollary of this is: Can there be too much organic matter?

This second question is not of practical consequence for biological grain/livestock farmers because it is almost financially impossible to raise organic matter levels on farm soils to extraordinary amounts. Large-scale holistic farmers must grow their own humus on their own farm. Their focus cannot be on buying and bringing in large quantities of organic matter; it must be on conserving and maximizing the value of the organic matter they produce themselves.

Where you do hear of an organic farmer (not vegetable grower but cereal/livestock farmer) building extraordinary fertility by spreading large quantities of compost, remember that this farmer must be located near an inexpensive source of quality material. If all the farmers wanted to do the same there would not be enough to go around at an economic price unless, perhaps, the entire country became a "closed system" like China. We would have to compost every bit of human excrement and organic matter and there still wouldn't be enough to meet the demand. Even if we became as efficient as China, keep in mind the degraded state of China's upland soils and the rapid desertification going on in their semi-arid west. China is robbing Peter to pay Paul and may not have a truly sustainable agriculture either.

I've frequently encountered a view among devotees of the organic gardening movement that if a little organic matter is a good thing, then more must be better and even more better still. In *Organic Gardening* magazine and Rodale garden books we read eulogies to soils that are so high in humus and so laced with earthworms that one can easily shove their arm into the soft earth elbow deep but must yank it out fast before all the hairs have been chewed off by worms, where one must jump away after planting corn seeds lest the stalk poke you in the eye, where the pumpkins average over 100 pounds each, where a single trellised tomato vine covers the entire south side of a house and yields bushels. All due to compost.

I call believers of the organic faith capital "O" organic gardeners. These folks almost inevitably have a pickup truck used to gather in their neighborhood's leaves and grass clippings on trash day and to haul home loads from local stables and chicken ranches. Their large yards are ringed with compost bins and their annual spreadings of compost are measured in multiples of inches. I was one once, myself.

There are two vital and slightly disrespectful questions that should be asked about this extreme of gardening practice. Is this much humus the only way to grow big, high-yielding organic vegetable gardens and two, are vegetables raised on soils super-high in humus maximally nutritious. If the answer to the first question is no, then a person might avoid a lot of work by raising the nutrient level of their soil in some other manner acceptable to the organic gardener. If the answer to the second question is less nutritious, then serious gardeners and homesteaders who are making home-grown produce into a significant portion of their annual caloric intake had better reconsider their health assumptions. A lot of organic gardeners cherish ideas similar to the character Woody Allen played in his movie, *Sleeper*.

Do you recall that movie? It is about a contemporary American who, coming unexpectedly close to death, is frozen and then reanimated and healed 200 years in the future. However, our hero did not expect to die or be frozen when he became ill and upon awakening believes the explanation given to him is a put on and that his friends are conspiring to make him into a fool. The irritated doctor in charge tells Woody to snap out of it and be prepared to start a new life. This is no joke, says the doctor, all of Woody's friends are long since dead. Woody's response is a classic line that earns me a few chuckles from the audience every time I lecture: "all my friends can't be dead! I owned a health food store and we all ate brown rice.'

Humus and the Nutritional Quality of Food

I believe that the purpose of food is not merely to fill the belly or to provide energy, but to create and maintain health. Ultimately, soil fertility should be evaluated not by humus content, nor microbial populations, nor earthworm numbers, but by the long-term health consequences of eating the food. If physical health degenerates, is maintained, or is improved we have measured the soil's true worth. The technical name for this idea is a "biological assay." Evaluating soil fertility by biological assay is a very radical step, for connecting long-term changes in health with the nutritional content of food and then with soil management practices invalidates a central tenet of industrial farming: that bulk yield is the ultimate measure of success or failure. As Newman Turner, an English dairy farmer and disciple of Sir Albert Howard, put it:

> The orthodox scientist normally measures the fertility of a soil by its bulk yield, with no relation to effect on the ultimate consumer.
>
> I have seen cattle slowly lose condition and fall in milk yield when fed entirely on the abundant produce of an apparently fertile soil. Though the soil was capable of yielding heavy crops, those crops were not adequate in themselves to maintain body weight and milk production in the cow, without supplements. That soil, though capable of above-average yields, and by the orthodox quantitative measure

regarded as fertile, could not, by the more complete measure of ulti-mate effect on the consumer, be regarded but anything but deficient in fertility.

Fertility therefore, is the ability to produce at the highest recognized level of yield, crops of quality which, when consumed over long periods by animals or man, enable them to sustain health, bodily condition and high level of production without evidence of disease or deficiency of any kind.

Fertility cannot be measured quantitatively. Any measure of soil fertility must be related to the quality of its produce.... The most simple measure of soil fertility is its ability to transmit, through its produce, fertility to the ultimate consumer.

Howard also tells of creating a super-healthy herd of work oxen on his research farm at Indore, India. After a few years of meticulous composting and restoration of soil life, Howard's oxen glowed with well-being. As a demonstration he intentionally allowed his animals to rub noses across the fence with neighboring oxen known to be infected with hoof and mouth and other cattle plagues. His animals remained healthy. I have read so many similar accounts in the liter-ature of the organic farming movement that in my mind there is no denying the relationship between the nutritional quality of plants and the presence of organic matter in soil. Many other organic gardeners reach the same conclusion. But most gardeners do not understand one critical difference between farming and gardening: most agricultural radicals start farming on run-down land grossly deficient in organic matter. The plant and animal health improvements they describe come from restoration of soil balance, from approaching a climax humus level much like I've done in my pasture by no longer removing the grass.

But home gardeners and market gardeners near cities are able to get their hands on virtually unlimited quantities of organic matter. Encour-aged by a mistaken belief that the more organic matter the healthier, they enrich their soil far beyond any natural capacity. Often this is called "building up the soil." But increasing organic matter in gardens well above a climax ecology level does not further increase the nutritional value of vegetables and in many circumstances will decrease their value markedly.

For many years I have lectured on organic gardening to the Extension Service's master gardener classes. Part of the master gardener training includes interpreting soil test results. In the early 1980s when Oregon State government had more money, all master gardener trainees were given a free soil test of their own garden. Inevitably, an older gentlemen would come up after my lecture and ask my interpretation of his puzzling soil test.

Ladies, please excuse me. Lecturing in this era of women's lib I've broken my politically incorrect habit of saying "the gardener, he ..." but in this case it *was* always a man, an organic gardener who had been building up his soil for years.

The average soils in our region test moderately to strongly acid; are low in nitrogen, phosphorus, calcium, and magnesium; quite adequate in potassium; and have 3–4 percent organic matter. Mr. Organic's soil test showed an organic matter content of 15 to 20 percent with more than adequate nitrogen and a pH of 7.2. However there was virtually no phosphorus, calcium or magnesium and four times the amount of potassium that any farm agent would ever recommend. On the bottom of the test, always written in red ink, underlined, with three exclamation points, "No more wood ashes for five years!!!" Because so many people in the Maritime northwest heat with firewood, the soil tester had mistakenly assumed that the soil became alkaline and developed such a potassium imbalance from heavy applications of wood ashes.

This puzzled gardener couldn't grasp two things about his soil test report. One, he did not use wood ashes and had no wood stove and two, although he had been "building up his soil for six or seven years," the garden did not grow as well as he had imagined it would. Perhaps you see why this questioner was always a man. Mr. Organic owned a pickup and loved to haul organic matter and to make and spread compost. His soil was full of worms and had a remarkably high humus level but still did not grow great crops.

It was actually worse than he understood. Plants uptake as much potassium as there is available in the soil, and concentrate that potassium in their top growth. So when vegetation is hauled in and composted or when animal manure is imported, large quantities of potassium come along with them. As will be explained shortly, vegetation from forested regions like western Oregon is even more potassium-rich and contains less of other vital nutrients than vegetation from other areas. By covering his soil several inches thick with manure and compost every year he had totally saturated the earth with potassium. Its cation exchange capacity or in non-technical language, the soil's ability to hold other nutrients had been overwhelmed with potassium and all phosphorus, calcium, magnesium, and other nutrients had largely been washed away by rain. It was even worse than that! The nutritional quality of the vegetables grown on that super humusy soil was very, very low and would have been far higher had he used tiny amounts of compost and, horror of all horrors, chemical fertilizer.

Climate and the Nutritional Quality of Food

Over geologic time spans, water passing through soil leaches or removes plant nutrients. In climates where there is barely enough rain to grow cereal crops, soils retain their minerals and the food produced there tends to be highly nutritious. In verdant, rainy climates the soil is leached of plant nutrients and the food grown there is much less nutritious. That's why the great healthy herds of animals were found on scrubby, semi-arid grasslands like the American prairies; in comparison, lush forests carry far lower quantities of animal biomass.

Some plant nutrients are much more easily leached out than others. The first valuable mineral to go is calcium. Semi-arid soils usually still retain large quantities of calcium. The nutrient most resistant to leaching is potassium. Leached out forest soils usually still retain relatively large amounts of potassium. William Albrecht observed this data and connected with it a number of fairly obvious and vital changes in plant nutritional qualities that are caused by these differences in soil fertility. However obvious they may be, Albrecht's work was not considered politically correct by his peers or the interest groups that supported agricultural research during the mid-twentieth century and his contributions have been largely ignored. Worse, his ideas did not quite fit with the ideological preconceptions of J.l. Rodale, so organic gardeners and farmers are also ignorant of Albrecht's wisdom.

Soil Mineral Content by Climate Area

Plant Nutrient	Dryland Prairie Soil	Humid Forest Soil
nitrogen	high	low
phosphorus	high	low
potassium	high	moderately high
calcium	very high	low
pH	neutral	acid

Dryland soils contain far higher levels of all minerals than leached soils. But Albrecht speculated that the key difference between these soils is the *ratio* of calcium to potassium. In dryland soils there is much more calcium in the soil than there is potassium while in wetter soils there is as much or more potassium than calcium. To test his theory he grew some soybeans in pots. One pot had soil with a high amount of calcium relative to the amount of potassium, imitating dryland prairie soil. The other pot had just as much calcium but had more potassium, giving it a ratio similar to a high quality farm soil in the eastern United States. Both soils grew good-looking samples of soybean plants, but when they were analyzed for nutritional content they proved to be quite different.

The potassium-fortified soil gave a 25 percent higher bulk yield but the soybeans contained 25 percent less protein. The consumer of those plants would have to burn off approximately 30 percent more carbohydrates to obtain the same amount of vital amino acids essential to all bodily functions. Wet-soil plants also contain only one-third as much calcium, an essential nutrient, whose lack over several generations causes gradual reduction of skeletal size and dental deterioration. They also contain only half as much phosphorus, another essential nutrient. Their oversupply of potassium is not needed; humans eating balanced diets usually excrete large quantities of unnecessary potassium in their urine.

Soil	Yield	Calories	Protein	Ca	P	K
Humid	17.8 gm	High	13%	0.27%	0.14%	2.15%
Dryland	14.7 gm	Medium	17%	0.74%	0.25%	1.01%

Albrecht then analyzed dozens of samples of vegetation that came from both dryland soils and humid soils and noticed differences in them similar to the soybeans grown under controlled conditions. The next chart, showing the average composition of plant vegetation from the two different regions, is taken directly from Albrecht's research. The figures are averages of large numbers of plant samples, including many different food crops from each climate.

Average Nutritional Content by Climate

Nutrient	Dryland Soil	Humid Soil
Potassium	2.44%	1.27%
Calcium	1.92%	0.28%
Phosphorus	0.78%	0.42%
Total mineral nutrition	5.14%	1.97%
Ratio of Potassium to Calcium	1.20:1	4.50:1

Analyzed as a whole, these data tell us a great deal about how we should manage our soil to produce the most nutritious food and about the judicious use of compost in the garden as well. I ask you to refer back to these three small charts as I point out a number of conclusions that can be drawn from them.

The basic nutritional problem that all animals have is not about finding energy food, but how to intake enough vitamins, minerals and usable proteins. What limits our ability to intake nutrients is the amount of bulk we can process—or the number of calories in the food. With cows, for example, bulk is the limiter. The cow will completely fill her digestive tract at all times and will process all the vegetation she can digest every day of her life. Her health depends on the amount of nutrition in that bulk. With humans, our modern lifestyle limits most of us to consuming 1,500 to 1,800 calories a day. Our health depends on the amount of nutrients coming along with those calories.

So I write the fundamental equation for human health as follows:

$$\text{Health} = \text{Nutrition in Food} \div \text{Calories in that Food}$$

If the food that we eat contains all of the nutrients that food could possibly contain, and in the right ratios, then we will get sufficient nutrition while consuming the calories we need to supply energy. However, to the degree that our diet contains denatured food supplying too much energy, we will be lacking nutrition and our bodies will suffer gradual degeneration. This is why foods such as sugar and fat are less healthful because they are concentrated sources of energy that contain little or no nutrition. Nutritionless food also contributes to "hidden hungers" since the organism craves something that is missing. The body overeats, and becomes fat and unhealthy.

Albrecht's charts show us that food from dry climates tends to be high in proteins and essential minerals while simultaneously lower in calories. Food from wet climates tends to be higher in calories while much lower in protein and essential mineral nutrients. Albrecht's writings, as well as those of Weston Price, and Sir Robert McCarrison listed in the bibliography, are full of examples showing how human health and longevity are directly associated with these same variations in climate, soil, and food nutrition.

Albrecht pointed out a clear example of soil fertility causing health or sickness. In 1940, when America was preparing for World War II, all eligible men were called in for a physical examination to determine fitness for military service. At that time, Americans did not eat the same way we do now. Food was produced and distributed locally. Bread was milled from local flour. Meat and milk came from local farmers. Vegetables and potatoes did not all come from California. Regional differences in soil fertility could be seen reflected in the health of people.

Albrecht's state, Missouri, is divided into a number of distinct rainfall regions. The northwestern part is grassy prairie and receives much less moisture than the humid, forested southeastern section. If soil tests were compared across a diagonal line drawn from the northwest to the southeast, they would exactly mimic the climate-caused mineral profile differences Albrecht had identified. Not unexpectedly, 200 young men per 1,000 draftees were medically unfit for military service from the northwest part of Missouri while 400 per 1,000 were unfit from the southeastern part. And 300 per 1,000 were unfit from the center of the state.

Another interesting, and rather frightening, conclusion can be drawn from the second chart. Please notice that by increasing the amount of potassium in the potting soil, Albrecht increased the overall yield by 25 percent while simultaneously lowering all of the other significant nutritional aspects. Most of this increase of yield was in the form of carbohydrates, that in a food crops equates to calories. Agronomists also know that adding potassium fertilizer greatly and inexpensively increases yield. So American farm soils are routinely dosed with potassium fertilizer, increasing bulk yield and profits without consideration for nutrition, or for the ultimate costs in public health. Organic farmers often do not understand this aspect of plant nutrition either and may use "organic" forms of potassium to increase their yields and profits. Buying organically grown food is no guarantee that it contains the ultimate in nutrition.

So, if health comes from paying attention to the ratio of nutrition to calories in our food, then as gardeners who are in charge of creating a significant amount of our own fodder, we can take that equation a step further:

Health = Nutrition ÷ Calories = Calcium ÷ Potassium

When we decide how to manage our gardens we can take steps to imitate dryland soils by keeping potassium levels lower while maintaining higher levels of calcium.

Now take another close look at the third chart. Average vegetation from dryland soils contains slightly more potassium than calcium (1.2:1) while average vegetation from wetland soils contains many more times more potassium than calcium (4.5:1). When we import manure or vegetation into our garden or farm soils we are adding large quantities of potassium. Those of us living in rainy climates that were naturally forested have it much worse in this respect than those of us gardening on the prairies or growing irrigated gardens in desert climates because the very vegetation and manure we use to "build up" our gardens contains much more potassium while most of our soils already contain all we need and then some.

It should be clear to you why some organic gardeners receive the soil tests like the man at my lecture. Even the soil tester, although scientifically trained and university educated, did not appreciate the actual source of the potassium overdose. The tester concluded it must have been wood ashes when actually the potassium came from organic matter itself.

I conclude that organic matter is somewhat dangerous stuff whose use should be limited to the amount needed to maintain basic soil tilth and a healthy, complex soil ecology.

Fertilizing Gardens Organically

Scientists analyzing the connections between soil fertility and the nutritional value of crops have repeatedly remarked that the best crops are grown with compost and fertilizer. Not fertilizer alone and not compost alone. The best place for gardeners to see these data is Werner Schupan's book (listed in the bibliography).

But say the word "fertilizer" to an organic gardener and you'll usually raise their hackles. Actually there is no direct linkage of the words "fertilizer" and "chemical." A fertilizer is any concentrated plant nutrient source that rapidly becomes available in the soil. In my opinion, chemicals are the poorest fertilizers; organic fertilizers are far superior.

The very first fertilizer sold widely in the industrial world was guano. It is the naturally sun-dried droppings of nesting sea birds that accumulates in thick layers on rocky islands off the coast of South America. Guano is a potent nutrient source similar to dried chicken manure, containing large quantities of nitrogen, fair amounts of phosphorus, and smaller quantities of potassium. Guano is more potent than any other manure because sea birds eat ocean fish, a very high protein and highly mineralized food. Other potent organic fertilizers include seed meals; pure, dried chicken manure; slaughterhouse wastes; dried kelp and other seaweeds; and fish meal.

Composition of Organic Fertilizers

Material	% N	% P	% K
Alfalfa meal	2.5	0.5	2.1
Bone meal (raw)	3.5	21.0	0.2
Bone meal (steamed)	2.0	21.0	0.2
Chicken manure (pure, fresh)	2.6	1.25	0.75
Cottonseed meal	7.0	3.0	2.0
Blood meal	12.0	3.0	—
Fish meal	8.0	7.0	—
Greensand	—	1.5	7.0
Hoof and Horn	12.5	2.0	—
Kelp meal	1.5	0.75	4.9
Peanut meal	3.6	0.7	0.5
Tankage	11.0	5.0	—

Growing most types of vegetables requires building a level of soil fertility that is much higher than required by field crops like cereals, soybeans, cotton and sunflowers. Field crops can be acceptably productive on ordinary soils without fertilization. However, because we have managed our farm soils as depreciating industrial assets rather than as relatively immortal living bodies, their ability to deliver plant nutrients has declined and the average farmer usually must add additional nutrients in the form of concentrated, rapidly-releasing fertilizers if they are going to grow a profitable crop.

Vegetables are much more demanding than field crops. They have long been adapted to growing on potent composts or strong manures like fresh horse manure or chicken manure. Planted and nourished like wheat, most would refuse to grow or if they did survive in a wheat field, vegetables would not produce the succulent, tender parts we consider valuable.

Building higher than normal levels of plant nutrients can be done with large additions of potent compost and manure. In semi-arid parts of the country where vegetation holds a beneficial ratio of calcium to potassium food grown that way will be quite nutritious. In areas of heavier rainfall, increasing soil fertility to vegetable levels is accomplished better with fertilizers. The data in the previous section gives strong reasons for many gardeners to limit the addition of organic matter in soil to a level that maintains a healthy soil ecology and acceptable tilth. Instead of supplementing compost with low quality chemical fertilizers, I recommend making and using a complete organic fertilizer mix to increase mineral fertility.

Complete Organic Fertilizer

COF costs only a tiny fraction of the supermarket price of the vegetables it grows—if you buy the major ingredients in 50 pound bags. Farm/ranch suppliers are the most likely sources. If you should find COF ingredients at a garden shop they will almost inevitably be offered in small quantities at shockingly high prices per pound. If I were an urban gardener I would drive to a country store and stock up.

A fertilizer that puts the highest nutritional content into the vegetables it grows must provide roughly equal amounts of nitrogen (N), phosphorus (P), and potassium (K, from kalium, its Latin name). It would also supply substantial amounts of calcium (Ca) and sulfur (S) and *effective* quantities of iodine, manganese, copper, zinc, molybdenum, boron, etc. I stress the word "effective" because a lab analysis of many prepared fertilizers (printed on the package at a garden center) may show all these elements are present but when the numbers are crunched it becomes clear that the amounts are too small to make a nutritional difference. An ideal garden fertilizer would release most of its nutrients over a few months instead of in a few days. That way they don't wash out of the topsoil with the first excessive irrigation or heavy rain. It would be odorless, finely powdered, not burn leaves if a little got on them and would not poison plants or soil life if accidentally double-dosed. All this accurately describes COF.

COF is intended to be concocted by the gardener. Precise measurement is not essential. Proportions varying plus or minus 10 percent will work out to be exact enough. I prepare mine using two 5 gallon white plastic buckets. First I put all the ingredients listed below into one bucket and then blend them thoroughly by pouring back and forth between two buckets at least 8 times. Spread the entire amount of the recipe below over 100 square feet of growing bed or intended root zone. There is no absolute need to dig or rototill it in; it also can be left on the surface or shallowly hoed in.

COF for 100 square feet

Nitrogen
5 pounds of oilseed meal, such as cottonseed meal, soybean meal, canolaseed meal; or else 15 pounds of bagged chicken manure compost.

Calcium
If you live where the native vegetation was a forest, 2 pounds agricultural lime *(not dolomite)* and 1 pound agricultural gypsum

If you live where the original vegetation was treeless grassy prairie or desert scrub, no aglime. Instead, use 2 pounds agricultural gypsum.

Phosphorus

2 pounds colloidal (soft) rock phosphate, or high phosphate guano or bone meal. If you use chicken manure compost for nitrogen then reduce the amount of phosphate fertilizer by half.

Potassium

½ pound potassium sulfate. Do not use greensand as promoted in so many organic gardening books. Do not use muriate of potash, KCl. It is slightly less costly than potassium sulfate but muriate causes leaching of calcium and degrades flavor.

Trace Elements and Micronutrients

- Borax 20 gm or ¾ ounce

- Manganese sulfate 30 gm or 1 ounce

- Zinc sulfate 15 gm or ½ ounce

- Copper sulfate 15 gm or ½ ounce

- Sodium molybdate 0.6 gm or ⅛ kitchen measuring teaspoon

- 1 pound kelp meal

Chapter 10

Making Superior Compost

The potency of composts can vary greatly. Most municipal solid waste compost has a high carbon to nitrogen ratio and when tilled into soil temporarily provokes the opposite of a good growth response until soil animals and microorganisms consume most of the undigested paper. But if low-grade compost is used as a surface mulch on ornamentals, the results are usually quite satisfactory even if unspectacular.

If the aim of your own composting is to conveniently dispose of yard waste and kitchen garbage, the information in the first half of the book is all you need to know. If you need compost to make something that dependably GROWs plants like it was fertilizer, then this chapter is for you.

A Little History

Before the twentieth century, the fertilizers market gardeners used were potent manures and composts. The vegetable gardens of country folk also received the best manures and composts available while the field crops got the rest. So I've learned a great deal from old farming and market gardening literature about using animal manures. In previous centuries, farmers classified manures by type and purity. There was "long" and "short" manure, and then, there was the supreme plant growth stimulant, chicken manure.

Chicken manure was always highly prized but usually in short supply because preindustrial fowl weren't caged in factories or permanently locked in hen houses and fed scientifically formulated mixes. The chicken breed of that era was usually some type of bantam, half-wild, broody, protective of chicks, and capable of foraging. A typical pre-1900 small-scale chicken management system was to allow the flock free access to hunt their own meals in the barnyard and orchard, luring them into the coop at dusk with a bit of grain where they were protected from predators while sleeping helplessly. Some manure was collected from the hen house but most of it was dropped where it could not be gathered. The daily egg hunt was worth it because, before the era of pesticides, having chickens range through the orchard greatly reduced problems with insects in fruit.

The high potency of chicken manure derives from the chickens' low C/N diet: worms, insects, tender shoots of new grass, and other proteinaceous young greens and seeds. Twentieth-century chickens "living" in egg and meat factories must still be fed low C/N foods, primarily grains, and their manure is still potent. But anyone who has savored real free-range eggs with deep orange yokes from chickens on a proper diet cannot be happy with what passes for "eggs" these days.

Fertilizing with pure chicken manure is not very different than using ground cereal grains or seed meals. It is so concentrated that it might burn plant leaves like chemical fertilizer does and must be applied sparingly to soil. It provokes a marked and vigorous growth response. Two or three gallons of dry, pure fresh chicken manure are sufficient nutrition to GROW about 100 square feet of vegetables in raised beds to the maximum.

Exclusively incorporating pure chicken manure into a vegetable garden also results in rapid humus loss, just as though chemical fertilizers were used. Any fertilizing substance with a C/N below that of stabilized humus, be it a chemical or a natural substance, accelerates the decline in soil organic matter. That is because nitrate nitrogen, the key to constructing all protein, is usually the main factor limiting the population of soil microorganisms. When the nitrate level of soil is significantly increased, microbe populations increase proportionately and proceeds to eat organic matter at an accelerated rate.

That is why small amounts of chemical fertilizer applied to soil that still contains a reasonable amount of humus has such a powerful effect. Not only does the fertilizer itself stimulate the growth of plants, but fertilizer increases the microbial population. More microbes accelerate the breakdown of humus and even more plant nutrients are released as organic matter decays. And that is why holistic farmers and gardeners mistakenly criticize chemical fertilizers as being directly destructive of soil microbes. Actually, all fertilizers, chemical or organic, *indirectly* harm soil life, first increasing their populations to unsustainable levels that drop off markedly once enough organic matter has been eaten. Unless, of course, the organic matter is replaced.

Chicken manure compost is another matter. Mix the pure manure with straw, sawdust, or other bedding, compost it and, depending on the amount and quantity of bedding used and the time allowed for decomposition to occur, the resultant C/N will be around 12:1 or above. Any ripened compost around 12:1 still will GROW plants beautifully. Performance drops off as the C/N increases.

Since chicken manure was scarce, most pre-twentieth century market gardeners depended on seemingly unlimited supplies of "short manure," generally from horses. The difference between the "long" and the "short" manure was bedding. Long manure contained straw from the stall while short manure was pure street sweepings without adulterants. Hopefully, the straw portion of long manure had absorbed a quantity of urine.

People of that era knew the fine points of hay quality as well as people today know their gasoline. Horses expected to do a day's work were fed on grass or grass/clover mixes that had been cut and dried while they still had a high protein content. Leafy hay was highly prized while hay that upon close inspection revealed lots of stems and seed heads would be rejected by a smart buyer. The working horse's diet was supplemented with a daily ration of grain. Consequently, uncomposted fresh short manure probably started out with a C/N around 15:1. However, don't count on anything that good from horses these days. Most horses aren't worked daily so their fodder is often poor. Judging from the stemmy, cut-too-late grass hay our local horses have to try to survive on, if I could find bedding-free horse manure it would probably have a C/N more like 20:1. Manure from physically fit thoroughbred race horses is probably excellent.

Using fresh horse manure in soil gave many vegetables a harsh flavor so it was first composted by mixing in some soil (a good idea because otherwise a great deal of ammonia would escape the heap). Market gardeners raising highly demanding crops like cauliflower and celery amended composted short manure by the inches-thick layer. Lesser nutrient-demanding crops like snap beans, lettuce, and roots followed these intensively fertilized vegetables without further compost.

Long manures containing lots of straw were considered useful only for field crops or root vegetables. Wise farmers conserved the nitrogen and promptly composted long manures. After heating and turning the resulting C/N would probably be in a little below 20:1. After tilling it in, a short period of time was allowed while the soil digested this compost before sowing seeds. Lazy farmers spread raw manure load by load as it came from the barn and tilled it in once the entire field was covered. This easy method allows much nitrogen to escape as ammonia while the manure dries in the sun. Commercial vegetable growers had little use for long manure.

One point of this brief history lesson is GIGO: garbage in, garbage out. The finished compost tends to have a C/N that is related to the ingredients that built the heap. Growers of vegetables will wisely take note.

Anyone interested in learning more about preindustrial market gardening might ask their librarian to seek out a book called *French Gardening* by Thomas Smith, published in London about 1905. This fascinating little book was written to encourage British market gardeners to imitate the Parisian marciér, who skillfully earned top returns growing out-of-season produce on intensive, double-dug raised beds, often under glass hot or cold frames. Our trendy American Biodynamic French Intensive gurus obtained their inspiration from England through this tradition.

Curing the Heap

The easiest and most sure-fire improver of compost quality is time. Making a heap with predominantly low C/N materials inevitably results in potent compost if nitrate loss is kept to a minimum. But the C/N of almost any compost heap, even one starting with a high C/N will eventually lower itself. The key word here is *eventually*. The most dramatic decomposition occurs during the first few turns when the heap is hot. Many people, including writers of garden books, mistakenly think that the composting ends when the pile cools and the material no longer resembles what made up the heap. This is not true. As long as a compost heap is kept moist and is turned occasionally, it will continue to decompose. "Curing" or "ripening" are terms used to describe what occurs once heating is over.

A different ecology of microorganisms predominates while a heap is ripening. If the heap contains 5 to 10 percent soil, is kept moist, is turned occasionally so it stays aerobic, and has a complete mineral balance, considerable bacterial nitrogen fixation may occur.

Most gardeners are familiar with the microbes that nodulate the roots of legumes. Called rhizobia, these bacteria are capable of fixing large quantities of nitrate nitrogen in a short amount of time. Rhizobia tend to be inactive during hot weather because the soil itself is supplying nitrates from the breakdown of organic matter. Summer legume crops, like cowpeas and snap beans, tend to be net consumers of nitrates, not makers of more nitrates than they can use. Consider this when you read in carelessly researched garden books and articles about the advantages of interplanting legumes with other crops because they supposedly generate nitrates that "help" their companions.

But during spring or fall when lowered soil temperatures retard decomposition, rhizobia can manufacture from 80 to 200 pounds of nitrates per acre. Peas, clovers, alfalfa, vetches, and fava beans can all make significant contributions of nitrate nitrogen and smart farmers prefer to grow their nitrogen by green manuring legumes. Wise farmers also know that this nitrate, though produced in root nodules, is used by legumes to grow leaf and stem. So the entire legume must be tilled in if any net nitrogen gain is to be realized. This wise practice simultaneously increases organic matter.

Rhizobia are not capable of being active in compost piles, but another class of microbes is. Called azotobacteria, these free-living soil dwellers also make nitrate nitrogen. Their contribution is not potentially as great as rhizobia, but no special provision must be made to encourage azotobacteria other than maintaining a decent level of humus for them to eat, a balanced mineral supply that includes adequate calcium, and a soil pH between 5.75 and 7.25. A high-yielding crop of wheat needs 60–80 pounds of nitrates per acre. Corn and most vegetables can use twice that amount. Azotobacteria can make enough for wheat, though an average nitrate contribution under good soil conditions might be more like 30–50 pounds per year.

Once a compost heap has cooled, azotobacteria will proliferate and begin to manufacture significant amounts of nitrates, steadily lowering the C/N. And carbon never stops being digested, further dropping the C/N. The rapid phase of composting may be over in a few months, but ripening can be allowed to go on for many more months if necessary.

Feeding unripened compost to worms is perhaps the quickest way to lower C/N and make a potent soil amendment. Once the high heat of decomposition has passed and the heap is cooling, it is commonly invaded by red worms, the same species used for vermicomposting kitchen garbage. These worms would not be able to eat the high C/N material that went into a heap, but after heating, the average C/N has probably dropped enough to be suitable for them.

The municipal composting operation at Fallbrook, California makes clever use of this method to produce a smaller amount of high-grade product out of a larger quantity of low-grade ingredients. Mixtures of sewage sludge and municipal solid waste are first composted and after cooling, the half-done high C/N compost is shallowly spread out over crude worm beds and kept moist. More crude compost is added as the worms consume the waste, much like a household worm box. The worm beds gradually rise. The lower portion of these mounds is pure castings while the worm activity stays closer to the surface where food is available. When the beds have grown to about three feet tall, the surface few inches containing worms and undigested food are scraped off and used to form new vermicomposting beds. The castings below are considered finished compost. By laboratory analysis, the castings contain three or four times as much nitrogen as the crude compost being fed to the worms.

The marketplace gives an excellent indicator of the difference between their crude compost and the worm casts. Even though Fallbrook is surrounded by large acreages devoted to citrus orchards and row crop vegetables, the municipality has a difficult time disposing of the crude product. But their vermicompost is in strong demand.

Sir Albert Howard's Indore Method

Nineteenth-century farmers and market gardeners had much practical knowledge about using manures and making composts that worked like fertilizers, but little was known about the actual microbial process of composting until our century. As information became available about compost ecology, one brilliant individual, Sir Albert Howard, incorporated the new science of soil microbiology into his composting and by patient experiment learned how to make superior compost.

During the 1920s, Albert Howard was in charge of a government research farm at Indore, India. At heart a Peace Corps volunteer, he made Indore operate like a very representative Indian farm, growing all the main staples of the local agriculture: cotton, sugar cane, and cereals. The farm was powered by the same work oxen used by the surrounding farmers. It would have been easy for Howard to demonstrate better yields through high technology by buying chemical fertilizers or using seed meal wastes from oil extraction, using tractors, and growing new, high-yielding varieties that could make use of more intense soil nutrition. But these inputs were not affordable to the average Indian farmer and Howard's purpose was to offer genuine help to his neighbors by demonstrating methods they *could* easily afford and use.

In the beginning of his work at Indore, Howard observed that the district's soils were basically fertile but low in organic matter and nitrogen. This deficiency seemed to be due to traditionally wasteful practices concerning manures and agricultural residues. So Howard began developing methods to compost the waste products of agriculture, making enough high-quality fertilizer to supply the entire farm. Soon, Indore research farm was enjoying record yields without having insect or disease problems, and without buying fertilizer or commercial seed. More significantly, the work animals, fed exclusively on fodder from Indore's humus-rich soil, become invulnerable to cattle diseases. Their shining health and fine condition became the envy of the district.

Most significant, Howard contended that his method not only conserved the nitrogen in cattle manure and crop waste, not only conserved the organic matter the land produced, but also raised the processes of the entire operation to an ecological climax of maximized health and production. Conserving the manure and composting the crop waste allowed him to increase the soil's organic matter which increased the soil's release of nutrients from rock particles that further increased the production of biomass which allowed him to make even more compost and so on. What I have just described is not surprising, it is merely a variation on good farming that some humans have known about for millennia.

What was truly revolutionary was Howard's contention about increasing net nitrates. With gentle understatement, Howard asserted that his compost was genuinely superior to anything ever known before. Indore compost had these advantages: no nitrogen or organic matter was lost from the farm through mishandling of agricultural wastes; the humus level of the farm's soils increased to a maximum sustainable level; and, *the amount of nitrate nitrogen in the finished compost was higher than the total amount of nitrogen contained in the materials that formed the heap.* Indore compost resulted in a net gain of nitrate nitrogen. The compost factory was also a biological nitrate factory.

Howard published details of the Indore method in 1931 in a slim book called *The Waste Products of Agriculture.* The widely read book brought him invitations to visit plantations throughout the British Empire. It prompted farmers world-wide to make compost by the Indore method. Travel, contacts, and new awareness of the problems of European agriculture were responsible for Howard's decision to create an organic farming and gardening movement.

Howard repeatedly warned in *The Waste Products of Agriculture* that if the underlying fundamentals of his process were altered, superior results would not occur. That was his viewpoint in 1931. However, humans being what we are, it does not seem possible for good technology to be broadcast without each user trying to improve and adapt it to their own situation and understanding. By 1940, the term "Indore compost" had become a generic term for any kind of compost made in a heap without the use of chemicals, much as "Rototiller" has come to mean any motor-driven rotary tiller.

Howard's 1931 concerns were correct—almost all alterations of the original Indore system lessened its value—but Howard of 1941 did not resist this dilutive trend because in an era of chemical farming any compost was better than no compost, any return of humus better than none.

Still, I think it is useful to go back to the Indore research farm of the 1920s and to study closely how Albert Howard once made the world's finest compost, and to encounter this great man's thoughts before he became a crusading ideologue, dead set against any use of agricultural chemicals. A great many valuable lessons are still contained in *The Waste Products of Agriculture.* Unfortunately, even though many organic gardeners are familiar with the later works of Sir Albert Howard the reformer, Albert Howard the scientist and researcher, who wrote this book, is virtually unknown today.

At Indore, all available vegetable material was composted, including manure and bedding straw from the cattle shed, unconsumed crop residues, fallen leaves and other forest wastes, weeds, and green manures grown specifically for compost making. All of the urine from the cattle shed-in the form of urine earth—and all wood ashes from any source on the farm were also included. Being in the tropics, compost making went on year-round. Of the result, Howard stated that:

> *The product is a finely divided leaf mould, of high nitrifying power, ready for immediate use [without temporarily inhibiting plant growth]. The fine state of division enables the compost to be rapidly incorporated and to exert its maximum influence on a very large area of the internal surface of the soil.*

Howard stressed that for the Indore method to work reliably the carbon to nitrogen ratio of the material going into the heap must always be in the same range. Every time a heap was built the same assortment of crop wastes were mixed with the same quantities of fresh manure and urine earth. As with my bread-baking analogy, Howard insured repeatability of ingredients.

Any hard, woody materials—Howard called them "refractory"—must be thoroughly broken up before composting, otherwise the fermentation would not be vigorous, rapid, and uniform throughout the process. This mechanical softening up was cleverly accomplished without power equipment by spreading tough crop wastes like cereal straw or pigeon pea and cotton stalks out over the farm roads, allowing cartwheels, the oxen's hooves, and foot traffic to break them up.

Decomposition must be rapid and aerobic, but not too aerobic. And not too hot. Quite intentionally, Indore compost piles were not allowed to reach the highest temperatures that are possible. During the first heating cycle, peak temperatures were about 140°. After two weeks, when the first turn was made, temperatures had dropped to about 125°, and gradually declined from there. Howard cleverly restricted the air supply and thermal mass so as to "bank the fires" of decomposition. This moderation was his key to preventing loss of nitrogen. Provisions were made to water the heaps as necessary, to turn them several times, and to use a novel system of mass inoculation with the proper fungi and bacteria. I'll shortly discuss each of these subjects in detail. Howard was pleased that there was no need to accept nitrogen loss at any stage and that the reverse should happen. Once the C/N had dropped sufficiently, the material was promptly incorporated into the soil where nitrate nitrogen will be best preserved. But the soil is not capable of doing two jobs at once. It can't digest crude organic matter and simultaneously nitrify humus. Thus compost must be finished and completely ripe when it was tilled in so that

...there must be no serious competition between the last stages of decay of the compost and the work of the soil in growing the crop. This is accomplished by carrying the manufacture of humus up to the point when nitrification is about to begin. In this way the Chinese principle of dividing the growing of a crop into two separate processes—(1) the preparation of the food materials outside the field, and (2) the actual growing of the crop-can be introduced into general agricultural practice.

And because he actually lived on a farm, Howard especially emphasized that composting must be sanitary and odorless and that flies must not be allowed to breed in the compost or around the work cattle. Country life can be quite idyllic—without flies.

The Indore Compost Factory

At Indore, Howard built a covered, open-sided, compost-making factory that sheltered shallow pits, each 30 feet long by 14 feet wide by 2 feet deep with sloping sides. The pits were sufficiently spaced to allow loaded carts to have access to all sides of any of them and a system of pipes brought water near every one. The materials to be composted were all stored adjacent to the factory. Howard's work oxen were conveniently housed in the next building.

Soil and Urine Earth

Howard had been raised on an English farm and from childhood he had learned the ways of work animals and how to make them comfortable. So, for the ease of their feet, the cattle shed and its attached, roofed loafing pen had earth floors. All soil removed from the silage pits, dusty sweepings from the threshing floors, and silt from the irrigation ditches were stored near the cattle shed and used to absorb urine from the work cattle. This soil was spread about six inches deep in the cattle stalls and loafing pen. About three times a year it was scraped up and replaced with fresh soil, the urine-saturated earth then was dried and stored in a special covered enclosure to be used for making compost .

The presence of this soil in the heap was essential. First, the black soil of Indore was well supplied with calcium, magnesium, and other plant nutrients. These basic elements prevented the heaps from becoming overly acid. Additionally, the clay in the soil was uniquely incorporated into the heap so that it coated everything. Clay has a strong ability to absorb ammonia, preventing nitrogen loss. A clay coating also holds moisture. Without soil, "an even and vigorous mycelial growth is never quickly obtained." Howard said "the fungi are the storm troops of the composting process, and must be furnished with all the armament they need."

Crop Wastes

Crop wastes were protected from moisture, stored dry under cover near the compost factory. Green materials were first withered in the sun for a few days before storage. Refractory materials were spread on the farm's roads and crushed by foot traffic and cart wheels before stacking. All these forms of vegetation were thinly layered as they were received so that the dry storage stacks became thoroughly mixed. Care was taken to preserve the mixing by cutting vertical slices out of the stacks when vegetation was taken to the compost pits. Howard said the average C/N of this mixed vegetation was about 33:1. Every compost heap made year-round was built with this complex assortment of vegetation having the same properties and the same C/N.

Special preliminary treatment was given to hard, woody materials like sugarcane, millet stumps, wood shavings and waste paper. These were first dumped into an empty compost pit, mixed with a little soil, and kept moist until they softened. Or they might be soaked in water for a few days and then added to the bedding under the work cattle. Great care was taken when handling the cattle's bedding to insure that no flies would breed in it.

Manure

Though crop wastes and urine-earth could be stored dry for later use, manure, the key ingredient of Indore compost, had to be used fresh. Fresh cow dung contains bacteria from the cow's rumen that is essential to the rapid decomposition of cellulose and other dry vegetation. Without their abundant presence composting would not begin as rapidly nor proceed as surely.

Charging the Compost Pits

Every effort was made to fill a pit to the brim within one week. If there wasn't enough material to fill an entire pit within one week, then a portion of one pit would be filled to the top. To preserve good aeration, every effort was made to avoid stepping on the material while filling the pit. As mixtures of manure and bedding were brought out from the cattle shed they were thinly layered atop thin layers of mixed vegetation brought in from the dried reserves heaped up adjacent to the compost factory. Each layer was thoroughly wet down with a clay slurry made of three ingredients: water, urine-earth, and actively decomposing material from an adjacent compost pit that had been filled about two weeks earlier. This insured that every particle within the heap was moist and was coated with nitrogen-rich soil and the microorganisms of decomposition. Today, we would call this practice "mass inoculation."

Pits Versus Heaps

India has two primary seasons. Most of the year is hot and dry while the monsoon rains come from dune through September. During the monsoon, so much water falls so continuously that the earth becomes completely saturated. Even though the pits were under a roof, they would fill with water during this period. So in the monsoon, compost was made in low heaps atop the ground. Compared to the huge pits, their dimensions were smaller than you would expect: 7 x 7 feet at the top, 8 x 8 feet at the base and no more than 2 feet high. When the rains started, any compost being completed in pits was transferred to above-ground heaps when it was turned.

Howard was accomplishing several things by using shallow pits or low but very broad heaps. One, thermal masses were reduced so temperatures could not reach the ultimate extremes possible while composting. The pits were better than heaps because air flow was further reduced, slowing down the fermentation, while their shallowness still permitted sufficient aeration. There were enough covered pits to start a new heap every week.

Temperature Range in Normal Pit

Age in days	Temperature in °C
3	63
4	60
6	58
11	55
12	53
13	49
14	49
First Turn	
18	49
20	51
22	48
24	47
29	46

Temperature Range in Normal Pit

Age in days	Temperature in °C
Second Turn	
37	49
38	45
40	40
43	39
57	39
Third Turn	
61	41
66	39
76	38
82	36
90	33

Period in days for each fall of 5 °C

Temperature Range	No. of Days
65–60	4
60–55	7
55–50	1
50–45	25
45–40	2
40–35	44
35–30	14

Total: 97 days

The compost was turned three times: To insure uniform decomposition, to restore moisture and air, and to supply massive quantities of those types of microbes needed to take the composting process to its next stage. The first turn was at about sixteen days. A second mass inoculation equivalent to a few wheelbarrows full of 30 day old composting material was taken from an adjacent pit and spread thinly over the surface of the pit being turned. Then, one half of the pit was dug out with a manure fork and placed atop the first half. A small quantity of water was added, if needed to maintain moisture. Now the compost occupied half the pit, a space about 15 x 14 and was about three feet high, rising out of the earth about one foot. During the monsoons when heaps were used, the above-ground piles were also mass inoculated and then turned so as to completely mix the material, and as we do today, placing the outside material in the core and vice-versa.

One month after starting, or about two weeks after the first turn, the pit or heap would be turned again. More water would be added. This time the entire mass would be forked from one half the pit to the other and every effort would be made to fluff up the material while thoroughly mixing it. And a few loads of material were removed to inoculate a 15-day-old pit.

Another month would pass, or about two months after starting, and for the third time the compost would be turned and then allowed to ripen. This time the material is brought out of the pit and piled atop the earth so as to increase aeration. At this late stage there would be no danger of encouraging high temperatures but the increased oxygen facilitated nitrogen fixation. The contents of several pits might be combined to form a heap no larger than 10 x 10 at the base, 9 x 9 on top, and no more than 3½ feet high. Again, more water might be added. Ripening would take about one month. Howard's measurements showed that after a month's maturation the finished compost should be used without delay or precious nitrogen would be lost. However, keep in mind when considering this brief ripening period that the heap was already as potent as it could become. Howard's problem was not further improving the C/N, it was conservation of nitrogen.

The Superior Value of Indore Compost.

Howard said that finished Indore compost was twice as rich in nitrogen as ordinary farmyard manure and that his target was compost with a C/N of 10:1. Since it was long manure he was referring to, let's assume that the C/N of a new heap started at 25:1.

The C/N of vegetation collected during the year is highly variable. Young grasses and legumes are very high in nitrogen, while dried straw from mature plants has a very high C/N. If compost is made catch-as-catch-can by using materials as they come available, then results will be highly erratic. Howard had attempted to make composts of single vegetable materials like cotton residues, cane trash, weeds, fresh green sweet clover, or the waste of field peas. These experiments were always unsatisfactory. So Howard wisely mixed his vegetation, first withering and drying green materials by spreading them thinly in the sun to prevent their premature decomposition, and then taking great care to preserve a uniform mixture of vegetation types when charging his compost pits. Howard was surprised to discover that he could compost all the crop waste he had available with only half the urine earth and about one-quarter of the oxen manure he had available. But fresh manure and urine earth were essential.

During the 1920s a patented process for making compost with a chemical fertilizer called Adco was in vogue and Howard tried it. Of using chemicals he said:

The weak point of Adco is that it does nothing to overcome one of the great difficulties in composting, namely the absorption of moisture in the early stages. In hot weather in India, the Adco pits lose moisture so rapidly that the fermentation stops, the temperature becomes uneven and then falls. When, however, urine earth and cow-dung are used, the residues become covered with a thin colloidal film, which not only retains moisture but contains combined nitrogen and minerals required by the fungi. This film enables the moisture to penetrate the mass and helps the fungi to establish themselves. Another disadvantage of Adco is that when this material is used according to the directions, the carbon-nitrogen ratio of the final product is narrower than the ideal 10:1. Nitrogen is almost certain to be lost before the crop can make use of it.

Fresh cow manure contains digestive enzymes and living bacteria that specialize in cellulose decomposition. Having a regular supply of this material helped initiate decomposition without delay. Contributing large quantities of actively growing microorganisms through mass inoculation with material from a two-week-old pile also helped. The second mass inoculation at two weeks, with material from a month-old heap provided a large supply of the type of organisms required when the heap began cooling. City gardeners without access to fresh manure may compensate for this lack by imitating Howard's mass inoculation technique, starting smaller amounts of compost in a series of bins and mixing into each bin a bit of material from the one further along at each turning. The passive backyard composting container automatically duplicates this advantage. It simultaneously contains all decomposition stages and inoculates the material above by contact with more decomposed material below. Using prepared inoculants in a continuous composting bin is unnecessary.

City gardeners cannot readily obtain urine earth. Nor are American country gardeners with livestock likely to be willing to do so much work. Remember that Howard used urine earth for three reasons. One, it contained a great deal of nitrogen and improved the starting C/N of the heap. Second, it is thrifty. Over half the nutrient content of the food passing through cattle is discharged in the urine. But, equally important, soil itself was beneficial to the process. Of this Howard said, "[where] there may be insufficient dung and urine earth for converting large quantities of vegetable wastes which are available, the shortage may be made up by the use of nitrate of soda .... If such artificials are employed, it will be a great advantage to make use of soil." I am sure he would have made very similar comments about adding soil when using chicken manure, or organic concentrates like seed meals, as cattle manure substitutes.

Control of the air supply is the most difficult part of composting. First, the process must stay aerobic. That is one reason that single-material heaps fail because they tend to pack too tightly. To facilitate air exchange, the pits or heaps were never more than two feet deep. Where air was insufficient (though still aerobic) decay is retarded but worse, a process called denitrification occurs in which nitrates and ammonia are biologically broken down into gasses and permanently lost. Too much manure and urine-earth can also interfere with aeration by making the heap too heavy, establishing anaerobic conditions. The chart illustrates denitrification caused by insufficient aeration compared to turning the composting process into a biological nitrate factory with optimum aeration.

Making Indore Compost in Deep and Shallow Pits

	4 feet deep	2 feet deep
Material weight at start	4,500 lb.	4,514 lb.
Total nitrogen at start	31.25 lb.	29.12 lb.
Total nitrogen at end	29.49 lb.	32.36 lb.
Change in nitrogen	-1.76 lb.	+3.24 lb.
Percentage change in nitrogen	-6.1%	+11.1%

Finally, modern gardeners might reconsider limiting temperature during composting. India is a very warm climate with balmy nights most of the year. Heaps two or three feet high will achieve an initial temperature of about 145°. The purchase of a thermometer with a long probe and a little experimentation will show you the dimensions that will more-or-less duplicate Howard's temperature regimes in your climate with your materials.

Inoculants

Howard's technique of mass inoculation with large amounts of biologically active material from older compost heaps speeds and directs decomposition. It supplies large numbers of the most useful types of microorganisms so they dominate the heap's ecology before other less desirable types can establish significant populations. I can't imagine how selling mass inoculants could be turned into a business.

But just imagine that seeding a new heap with tiny amounts of superior microorganisms could speed initial decomposition and result in a much better product. That *could* be a business. Such an approach is not without precedent. Brewers, vintners, and bread makers all do that. And ever since composting became interesting to twentieth-century farmers and gardeners, entrepreneurs have been concocting compost starters that are intended to be added by the ounce(s) to the cubic yard.

Unlike the mass inoculation used at Indore, these inoculants are a tiny population compared to the microorganisms already present in any heap. In that respect, inoculating compost is very different than beer, wine, or bread. With these food products there are few or no microorganisms at the start. The inoculant, small as it might be, still introduces millions of times more desirable organisms than those wild types that might already be present.

But the materials being assembled into a new compost heap are already loaded with microorganism. As when making sauerkraut, what is needed is present at the start. A small packet of inoculant is not likely to introduce what is not present anyway. And the complex ecology of decomposition will go through its inevitable changes as the microorganisms respond to variations in temperature, aeration, pH, etc.

This is one area of controversy where I am comfortable seeking the advice of an expert. In this case, the authority is Clarence Golueke, who personally researched and developed U.C. fast composting in the early 1950s, and who has been developing municipal composting systems ever since. The bibliography of this book lists two useful works by Golueke.

Golueke has run comparison tests of compost starters of all sorts because, in his business, entrepreneurs are constantly attempting to sell inoculants to municipal composting operations. Of these vendors, Golueke says with thinly disguised contempt:

> *Most starter entrepreneurs include enzymes when listing the ingredients of their products. The background for this inclusion parallels the introduction of purportedly advanced versions of starters—i.e., "advanced" in terms of increased capacity, utility and versatility. Thus in the early 1950's (when [I made my] appearance on the compost scene), starters were primarily microbial and references to*

identities of constituent microbes were very vague. References to enzymes were extremely few and far between. As early ("pioneer") researchers began to issue formal and informal reports on microbial groups (e.g., actinomycetes) observed by them, they also began to conjecture on the roles of those microbial groups in the compost process. The conjectures frequently were accompanied by surmises about the part played by enzymes.

Coincidentally, vendors of starters in vogue at the time began to claim that their products included the newly reported microbial groups as well as an array of enzymes. For some reason, hormones were attracting attention at the time, and so most starters were supposedly laced with hormones. In time, hormones began to disappear from the picture, whereas enzymes were given a billing parallel to that accorded to the microbial component.

Golueke has worked out methods of testing starters that eliminates any random effects and conclusively demonstrates their result. Inevitably, and repeatedly, he found that there was no difference between using a starter and not using one. And he says:

Although anecdotal accounts of success due to the use of particular inoculum are not unusual in the popular media, we have yet to come across unqualified accounts of successes in the refereed scientific and technical literature.

I use a variation of mass inoculation when making compost. While building a new heap, I periodically scrape up and toss in a few shovels of compost and soil from where the previous pile was made. Frankly, if I did not do this I don't think the result would be any worse.

Bibliography

On composting and soil organic matter

Workshop on the Role of Earthworms in the Stabilization of Organic Residues, Vol. I and II. Edited by Mary Appelhof. Kalamazoo, Michigan: Beech Leaf Press of the Kalamazoo Nature Center, 1981. If ever there was a serious investigation into the full range of the earthworm's potential to help Homo Sapiens, this conference explored it. Volume II is the most complete bibliography ever assembled on the earthworm.

Appelhof, Mary. *Worms Eat My Garbage.* Kalamazoo, Michigan: Flower Press, 1982. A delightful, slim, easy reading, totally positive book that offers enthusiastic encouragement to take advantage of vermicomposting.

Barrett, Dr. Thomas J. *Harnessing the Earthworm.* Boston: Wedgewood Press, 1959.

The Biocycle Guide to the Art & Science of Composting. Edited by the Staff of *Biocycle: Journal of Waste Recycling.* Emmaus, Pennsylvania: J.G. Press, 1991. The focus of this book is on municipal composting and other industrial systems. Though imprinted "Emmaus" this is not the Rodale organization, but a group that separated from Rodale Press over ten years ago. Included on the staff are some old *Organic Gardening and Farming* staffers from the 1970s, including Gene Logsdon and Jerome Goldstein. A major section discussing the biology and ecology of composting is written by Clarence Golueke. There are articles about vermicomposting, anaerobic digestion and biogasification, and numerous descriptions of existing facilities.

Campbell, Stu. *Let It Rot!* Pownal, Vermont: Storey Communications, Inc., 1975. Next to my book, the best in-print at-home compost making guide.

Darwin, Charles R. *The Formation of Vegetable Mould through the Action of Worms with Observations on their Habits.* London: John Murray & Co., 1881.

Dindal, Daniel L. *Ecology of Compost.* Syracuse, New York: N.Y. State Council of Environmental Advisors and SUNY College of Environmental Science and Forestry, 1972. Actually, a little booklet but very useful.

Golueke, Clarence G., Ph.D. *Composting: A Study of the Process and its Principles.* Emmaus: Rodale Press, 1972. Golueke, writing in "scientific" says much of what my book does in one-third as many words that are three times as long. He is America's undisputed authority on composting.

Hopkins, Donald P. *Chemicals, Humus and the Soil.* Brooklyn: Chemical Publishing Company, 1948. Any serious organic gardener should confront Donald Hopkins' thoughtful critique of Albert Howard's belief system. This book demolishes the notion that chemical fertilizers are intrinsically harmful to soil life while correctly stressing the vital importance of humus.

Hopp, Henry. *What Every Gardener Should Know About Earthworms.* Charlotte, Vermont: Garden Way Publishing Company, 1973. Hopp was a world-recognized expert on the earthworm.

Howard, Albert. *An Agricultural Testament.* London & New York: Oxford University Press, 1940. Describes Howard's early crusade to restore humus to industrial farming.

Howard, Albert. *The Soil and Health.* New York: Devin Adair, 1947. Also published in London by Faber & Faber, titled *Farming and Gardening for Health or Disease.* A full development of Howard's theme that humus is health for plants, animals and people.

Howard, Albert and Yeshwant D. Wad. *The Waste Products of Agriculture: Their Utilization as Humus.* London: Oxford University Press, 1931. Many organic gardeners have read Howard's *An Agricultural Testament*, but almost none have heard of this book. It is the source of my information about the original Indore composting system.

Howard, Louise E. *The Earth's Green Carpet.* Emmaus: Rodale Press, 1947. An oft-overlooked book by Howard's second wife. This one, slim volume expresses with elegant and passionate simplicity all of the basic beliefs of the organic gardening and farming movement. See also her *Albert Howard in India.*

Kevan, D. Keith. *Soil Animals.* London: H. F. & G. Witherby Ltd., 1962. Soil zoology for otherwise well-schooled layreaders.

King, F.H. *Farmers of Forty Centuries or Permanent Agriculture in China, Korea and Japan.* Emmaus: Rodale Press, first published 1911. Treasured by the organic gardening movement for its description of a long-standing and successful agricultural system based completely on composting. It is a great travel/adventure book.

Koepf, H.H., B.D. Petterson, and W. Shaumann. *Bio-Dynamic Agriculture: An Introduction.* Spring Valley, New York: Anthroposophic Press, 1976. A good introduction to this philosophical/mystical system of farming and gardening that uses magical compost inoculants.

Krasilnikov, N A. *Soil Microorganisms and Higher Plants.* Translated by Y.A. Halperin. Jerusalem: Israel Program for Scientific Translations, 1961. Organic gardeners have many vague beliefs about how humus makes plants healthy. This book scientifically explains why organic matter in soil makes plants healthy. Unlike most translations of Russian, this one is an easy read.

Kühnelt, Wilhelm. *Soil Biology: with special reference to the animal kingdom.* East Lansing: Michigan State University Press, 1976. Soil zoology at a level assuming readers have university- level biology, zoology and microbiology. Still, very interesting to well-read lay persons who are not intimidated by Latin taxonomy.

Minnich, Jerry. *The Earthworm Book: How to Raise and Use Earthworms for Your Farm and Garden.* Emmaus: Rodale Press, 1977. This book is a thorough and encyclopedic survey of the subject.

Minnich, Jerry and Marjorie Hunt. *The Rodale Guide to Composting.* Emmaus, Pennsylvania: Rodale Press, 1979. A very complete survey of composting at home, on the farm, and in municipalities. The book has been through numerous rewritings since the first edition; this version is the best. It is more cohesive and less seeming like it was written by a committee than the version in print now. *Organic Gardening and Farming* magazine may have been at its best when Minnich was a senior editor.

Oliver, George Sheffield. *Our Friend the Earthworm.* Library no. 26. Emmaus: Rodale Press, 1945. During the 1940s Rodale Press issued an inexpensive pamphlet library; this is one of the series.

Pfeiffer, E.E. *Biodynamic Farming and Gardening.* Spring Valley, New York: Anthroposophic Press, 1938.

Poincelot, R.P. *The Biochemistry and Methodology of Composting.* Vol. Bull. 727. Conn. Agric. Expt. Sta., 1972. A rigorous but readable review of scientific literature and known data on composting through 1972 including a complete bibliography.

Russell, Sir E. John. *Soil Conditions and Plant Growth.* Eighth Ed., New York: Longmans, Green & Co., 1950. The best soil science text I know of. Avoid the recent in-print edition that has been revised by a committee of current British agronomists. They enlarged Russell's book and made more credible to academics by making it less comprehensible to ordinary people with good education and intelligence through the introduction of unnecessary mathematical models and stilted prose. it lacks the human touch and simpler explanations of Russell's original statements.

Schaller, Friedrich. *Soil Animals.* Ann Arbor: University of Michigan, 1968. Soil zoology for American readers without extensive scientific background. Shaler was Kühnelt's student.

Stout, Ruth. *Gardening Without Work: For the Aging, the Busy and the Indolent.* Old Greenwich, Connecticut: Devin Adair, 1961. The original statement of mulch gardening. Fun to read. Her disciple, Richard Clemence, wrote several books in the late 1970s that develop the method further.

Of interest to the serious food gardener

I have learned far more from my own self-directed studies than my formal education. From time to time I get enthusiastic about some topic and voraciously read about it. When I started gardening in the early 1970s I quickly devoured everything labeled "organic" in the local public library and began what became a ten-year subscription to *Organic Gardening and Farming* magazine. During the early 1980s the garden books that I wrote all had the word "organic" in the title.

In the late 1980s my interest turned to what academics might call "the intellectual history of radical agriculture." I reread the founders of the organic gardening and farming movement, only to discover that they, like Mark Twain's father, had become far more intelligent since I last read them fifteen years back. I began to understand that one reason so many organic gardeners misunderstood Albert Howard was that he wrote in English, not American. I also noticed that there were other related traditions of agricultural reform and followed these back to their sources. This research took over eighteen months of heavy study. I really gave the interlibrary loan librarian a workout.

Herewith are a few of the best titles I absorbed during that research. I never miss an opportunity to help my readers discover that older books were written in an era before all intellectuals were afflicted with lifelong insecurity caused by cringing from an imaginary critical and nattery college professor standing over their shoulder. Older books are often far better than new ones, especially if you'll forgive them an occasional error in point of fact. We are not always discovering newer, better, and improved. Often we are forgetting and obscuring and confusing what was once known, clear and simple. Many of these extraordinary old books are not in print and not available at your local library. However, a simple inquiry at the Interlibrary Loan desk of most libraries will show you how easy it is to obtain these and most any other book you become interested in.

Albrecht, William A. *The Albrecht Papers, Vols 1 &2.* Kansas City: Acres, USA 1975. Albert Howard, Weston Price, Sir Robert Mc-Carrison, and William Albrecht share equal responsibility for creating this era's movement toward biologically sound agriculture. Howard is still well known to organic gardeners, thanks to promotion by the Rodale organization while Price, McCarrison, and Albrecht have faded into obscurity. Albrecht was chairman of the Soil Department at the University of Missouri during the 1930s. His unwavering investigation of soil fertility as the primary cause of health and disease was considered politically incorrect by the academic establishment and vested interests that funded agricultural research at that time. Driven from academia, he wrote prolifically for nonscientific magazines and lectured to farmers and medical practitioners during the 1940s and 1950s. Albrecht was willing to consider chemical fertilizers as potentially useful though he did not think chemicals were as sensible as more natural methods. This view was unacceptable to J.l. Rodale, who ignored Albrecht's profound contributions.

Balfour, Lady Eve B. *The Living Soil.* London: Faber and Faber, 1943. Lady Balfour was one of the key figures in creating the organic gardening and farming movement. She exhibited a most remarkable intelligence and understanding of the science of health and of the limitations of her own knowledge. Balfour is someone any serious gardener will want to meet through her books. Lady Balfour proved Woody Allen right about eating organic brown rice; she died only recently in her late 90s, compus mentis to the end.

Borsodi, Ralph. *Flight from the City: An Experiment in Creative Living on the Land.* New York: Harper and Brothers, 1933. A warmly human back-to-the-lander whose pithy critique of industrial civilization still hits home. Borsodi explains how production of life's essentials at home with small-scale technology leads to enhanced personal liberty and security. Homemade is inevitably more efficient, less costly, and better quality than anything mass-produced. Readers who become fond of this unique individualist's sociology and political economy will also enjoy Borsodi's *This Ugly Civilization* and *The Distribution Age*.

Brady, Nyle C. *The Nature and Properties of Soils,* Eighth Edition. New York: Macmillan, 1974. Through numerous editions and still the standard soils text for American agricultural colleges. Every serious gardener should attempt a reading of this encyclopedia of soil knowledge every few years. See also Foth, Henry D. *Fundamentals of Soil Science.*

Bromfield, Louis. *Malibar Farm.* New York: Harper & Brothers, 1947. Here is another agricultural reformer who did not exactly toe the Organic Party line as promulgated by J.l. Rodale. Consequently his books are relatively unknown to today's gardening public. If you like Wendell Berry you'll find Bromfield's emotive and lyrical prose even finer and less academically contrived. His experiments with ecological farming are inspiring. See also Bromfield's other farming books: *Pleasant Valley, In My Experience,* and *Out of the Earth.*

Carter, Vernon Gill and Dale, Tom. *Topsoil and Civilization.* Norman: University of Oklahoma Press, 1974. (first edition, 1954) This book surveys seven thousand years of world history to show how each place where civilization developed was turned into an impoverished, scantily-inhabited semi-desert by neglecting soil conservation. Will ours' survive any better? Readers who wish to pursue this area further might start with Wes Jackson's *New Roots for Agriculture.*

Ernle, (Prothero) Lord. *English Farming Past and Present,* 6th edition. First published London: Longmans, Green & Co., Ltd., 1912, and many subsequent editions. Chicago: Quadrangle Books, 1962. Some history is dry as dust. Ernle's writing lives like that of Francis Parkman or Gibbon. Anyone serious about vegetable gardening will want to know all they can about the development of modern agricultural methods.

Foth, Henry D. *Fundamentals of Soil Science,* Eighth Edition. New York: John Wylie & Sons, 1990. Like Brady's text, this one has also been through numerous editions for the past several decades. Unlike Brady's work however, this book is a little less technical, an easier read as though designed for non-science majors. Probably the best starter text for someone who wants to really understand soil.

Hall, Bolton. *Three Acres and Liberty.* New York: Macmillan, 1918. Bolton Hall marks the start of our modern back-to-the- land movement. He was Ralph Borsodi's mentor and inspiration. Where Ralph was smooth and intellectual, Hall was crusty and Twainesque.

Hamaker, John. D. *The Survival of Civilization.* Annotated by Donald A. Weaver. Michigan/ California: Hamaker-Weaver Publishers, 1982. Forget global warming, Hamaker believably predicts the next ice age is coming. Glaciers will be upon us sooner than we know unless we reverse intensification of atmospheric carbon dioxide by remineralization of the soil. Very useful for its exploration of the agricultural use of rock flours. Helps one stand back from the current global warming panic and ask if we really know what is coming. Or are we merely feeling guilty for abusing Earth?

Hopkins, Cyril G. *Soil Fertility and Permanent Agriculture.* Boston: Ginn and Company, 1910. Though of venerable lineage, this book is still one of the finest of soil manuals in existence. Hopkins' interesting objections to chemical fertilizers are more economic than moral.

Hopkins, Cyril G. *The Story of the Soil: From the Basis of Absolute Science and Real Life.* Boston: Richard G. Badger, 1911. A romance of soil science similar to Ecotopia or Looking Backward. No better introduction exists to understanding farming as a process of management of overall soil mineralization. People who attempt this book should be ready to forgive that Hopkins occasionally expresses opinions on race and other social issues that were acceptable in his era but today are considered objectionable by most Americans.

Jenny, Hans. *Factors of Soil Formation: a System of Quantitative Pedology.* New York: McGraw Hill, 1941. Don't let the title scare you. Jenny's masterpiece is not hard to read and still stands in the present as the best analysis of how soil forms from rock. Anyone who is serious about growing plants will want to know this data.

McCarrison, Sir Robert. *The Work of Sir Robert McCarrison.* ed. H. M. Sinclair. London Faber and Faber, 1953. One of the forgotten discoverers of the relationship between soil fertility and human health. McCarrison, a physician and medical researcher, worked in India contemporaneously with Albert Howard. He spent years "trekking around the Hunza and conducted the first bioassays of food nutrition by feeding rat populations on the various national diets of India. And like the various nations of India, some of the rats became healthy, large, long-lived, and good-natured while others were small, sickly, irritable, and short-lived.

Nearing, Helen & Scott. *Living the Good Life: How to Live Sanely and Simply in a Troubled World.* First published in 1950. New York: Schocken Books, 1970. Continuing in Borsodi's footsteps, the Nearings homesteaded in the thirties and began proselytizing for the self-sufficient life-style shortly thereafter. Scott was a very dignified old political radical when he addressed my high school in Massachusetts in 1961 and inspired me to dream of country living. He remained active until nearly his hundredth birthday. See also: *Continuing the Good Life* and *The Maple Sugar Book.*

Parnes, Robert. *Organic and Inorganic Fertilizers.* Mt. Vernon, Maine: Woods End Agricultural Institute, 1986.

Price, Weston A. *Nutrition and Physical Degeneration.* La Mesa, California: Price-Pottenger Nutrition Foundation, reprinted 1970. (1939)

Sits on the "family bible" shelf in my home along with Albrecht, McCarrison, and Howard. Price, a dentist with strong interests in prevention, wondered why his clientele, 1920s midwest bourgeoisie, had terrible teeth when prehistoric skulls of aged unlettered savages retained all their teeth in perfect condition. So he traveled to isolated parts of the Earth in the early 1930s seeking healthy humans. And he found them— belonging to every race and on every continent. And found out why they lived long, had virtually no degeneration of any kind including dental degeneration. Full of interesting photographs, anthropological data, and travel details. A trail-blazing work that shows the way to greatly improved human health.

Rodale, J.I. *The Organic Front*. Emmaus: Rodale Press, 1948. An intensely ideological statement of the basic tenets of the Organic faith. Rodale established the organic gardening and farming movement in the United States by starting up *Organic Gardening and Farming* magazine in 1942. His views, limitations and preferences have defined "organic" ever since. See also: *Pay Dirt*.

Schuphan, Werner. *Nutritional Values in Crops and Plants*. London: Faber and Faber, 1965. A top-rate scientist asks the question: "Is organically grown food really more nutritious?" The answer is: "yes, and no."

Smith, J. Russell. *Tree Crops: A Permanent Agriculture*. New York: Harcourt, Brace and Company, 1929. No bibliography of agricultural alternatives should overlook this classic critique of farming with the plow. Delightfully original!

Solomon, Steve. *Growing Vegetables West of the Cascades*. Seattle, Washington: Sasquatch Books, 1989. My strictly regional focus combined with the reality that the climate west of the Cascades is radically different than the rest of the United States has made this vegetable gardening text virtually unknown to American gardeners east of the Cascades. It has been praised as the best regional garden book ever written. Its analysis of soil management, and critique of Rodale's version of the organic gardening and farming philosophy are also unique. I founded and ran Territorial Seed Company, a major, mail-order vegetable garden seed business; no other garden book has ever encompassed my experience with seeds and the seed world.

Solomon, Steve. *Water-Wise Gardening*. Good Books, 2022. How to grow vegetables without dependence on irrigation. Make your vegetables able to survive long periods of drought and still be very productive. My approach is extensive, old fashioned and contrarian, the opposite of today's intensive, modern, trendy postage-stamp living.

Turner, Frank Newman. *Fertility, Pastures and Cover Crops Based on Nature's Own Balanced Organic Pasture Feeds.* reprinted from: Faber and Faber, 1955. ed., San Diego: Rateaver, 1975. An encouragement to farm using long rotations and green manuring systems from a follower of Albert Howard. Turner offered a remarkably sensible definition for soil fertility, in essence, "if my livestock stay healthy, live long, breed well, and continue doing so for at least four generations, then my soil was fertile."

Voisin, Andre. *Better Grassland Sward*. London: Crosby Lockwood and Sons, Ltd., 1960. The first half is an amazing survey of the role of the earthworm in soil fertility. The rest is just Voisin continuing on at his amazing best. No one interested in soil and health should remain unfamiliar with Voisin's intelligence. See also: *Grass Tetany, Grass Productivity*, and *Soil, Grass and Cancer*.